Choosing to Learn

Ownership and Responsibility in a Primary Multiage Classroom

Penelle Chase
Jane Doan

HEINEMANN
Portsmouth, NH

Heinemann
A division of Reed Elsevier Inc.
361 Hanover Street
Portsmouth, NH 03801–3912
Offices and agents throughout the world

Acquisitions Editor: Toby Gordon
Production Editor: Renée M. Nicholls
Cover Designer: Linda Knowles
Manufacturing Coordinator: Elizabeth Valway

Library of Congress Cataloging-in-Publication Data

Chase, Penelle.
    Choosing to learn : ownership and responsibility in a primary multiage
classroom / Penelle Chase, Jane Doan.
        p.   cm.
    Includes bibliographical references (p.   ).
    ISBN 0–435–07223–4 (alk. paper)
    1. Education—Experimental methods.   2. Autonomy in children.
3. Decision making in children.   4. Learning.   5. Nongraded schools.
6. Education, Primary.   I. Doan, Jane.   II. Title.
LB1027.3.C53   1996
372.13'9—dc20   96–28534
                                                                      CIP

Printed in the United States of America on acid-free paper
99 98 97 96 EB 1 2 3 4 5 6

For Addison, Phoebe, and Meg
(P. C.)

In Memory of Peg
(J. D.)

Contents

Preface

Penelle Chase

For seven years Jane and I have cotaught a multiaged group of children ranging from five to eight years old. During the first several years of working together in this setting, we were caught up in researching the multiage aspects of the program. We were intent on the processes of building community and adjusting curriculum to meet the needs of the wide-ranging developmental levels of our learners. It was exciting in those first years to learn with our multiage family and to work at ironing out the wrinkles in the program. We wrote about these experiences in our book *Full Circle: A New Look at Multiage Education*.

As the ins and outs of teaching in our multiage classrooms became more routine for us, we began looking closely at the elements that made learning in this setting work so well. It seemed too easy. How *were* we managing to teach forty children of all these different ages the things they were supposed to be learning in the three- or four-year span of time they spent with us? The more we looked for answers within our own teaching practices, the more we found that the children themselves held the key. After all, they were doing the significant work in the classroom; they were the learners. We saw that they were the ones ultimately in control of their learning. It was becoming more and more apparent to us that our job was not to teach them, but to help them learn.

This scrutiny launched us on another bout of classroom research and reflection. This time our focus was on student ownership and responsibility. We present our discoveries in this second book. It is a book about allowing students to take charge of their learning. It is about ways children choose to become participants in their education.

Since we began our research, the issue of choice has confronted us often, both in and out of our classrooms. Recently I was looking through my notes, and I discovered two day-book entries that I had written in the early "gathering material" stages of our thinking about student choice. One entry is about my daughter Phoebe, who was then a junior in college. The other is about Lauren, who was a first-year student in our class at that time. As I reread my notes, I was struck by the similarities in the two girls' temperaments. I began to think about the opportunities for choice that each had experienced as students.

First, the entry about Phoebe.

Day Book Entry   November 9

Phoebe made a difficult choice recently in one of her courses. Several weeks ago she had spoken to me on the phone about an oral presentation that was coming up in her art history course. She was fretting about it then; presenting in front of others is terrifying for Phoebe. She dreads the idea of it so thoroughly, that I believe she makes herself sick beforehand. I asked her about this. Was it just stage fright? Didn't she feel satisfied when a presentation was over? Was she relieved and okay then? She said "no," that she always feels that she has presented poorly, and she continues to feel *bad*. I agonized with her, remembering my own incapacity to speak publicly when I was a student. I knew Phoebe's anxiety would continue to build as presentation time neared.

Phoebe and I talked again last night, and I got an update. In this case, Phoebe made a choice. She chose not to show up for class on presentation day. Instead, she saw the professor after class and told him that she was not willing to do an oral presentation. To his credit, he offered her an alternative—she could come and talk with him informally in his office at another time. In substance, he would allow her to do her presentation one-on-one. That is what Phoebe did. Last night on the phone, Phoebe reported that they had had a great talk. She felt comfortable, and the professor was able to see that she was well versed in the subject matter. She described her professor, "He is great. He doesn't think that people just learn in one way or show what they know in one way." Such an attitude is somewhat unique at Phoebe's college, where oral participation is highly valued.

I am pleased that Phoebe took the risk to make a choice—I suspect that unconsciously she realized that her professor would respect her choice. I think Phoebe's level of terror in regard to speaking makes it impossible for her to be a "presenter" at this point in her life. I think that eventually she will be able to speak in front of others. But pressuring her to do it before she is ready is not the answer—she will come to it when she can, and she will know when that time is. I am glad that her teacher allowed her to choose a way to share her knowledge that was possible for her.

I must continually remind myself to give students options for showing what they know. Sometimes I am frustrated by the quiet ones in my class, their seeming lack of involvement. I want to call on them, to force them to become engaged in a vocal way. When I try such tactics and see the child floundering, I am disgusted with myself afterward. What if that was a little Phoebe sitting there feeling mortified?

Here are my notes about Lauren.

Day Book Entry   November 21

Every day at Choice Time Lauren signs up for a different choice. She comes to me each day saying that she doesn't know what the choices are. Then I ask her if she would like to ask one of the other children in the sign-up area to help her. She usually declines this suggestion (very sweetly), at which point I ask, "Who can help Lauren read the choices?" There are always several eager volunteers. Later, after Morning Meeting, Lauren almost always comes to me saying, "I can't remember what I signed up for." Then I go to the board with her to help her read the choice she has signed under, and she goes off to do that choice.

Often Lauren is alone at Choice Time. She never discusses choices with other children, who might encourage her to sign up with them. She just studies the choices and decides what she would like to try. Though many of the first-year students have experimented with Choice Time in Jane's room, Lauren almost always stays in my room. So far, she has not joined into the social scene much. After Lauren has been reminded of her choice, she does it contentedly until Choice Time is over. She has tried many more of the choices than the other first-year students. For the first several weeks she did painting, reading, writing, or drawing. Then she did the leaf rubbing and made a seed picture. Recently she has played with Legos and modeled with clay. If she chooses a "making" choice, she is always proud of the things she makes. She comes to me at the end of Choice Time and shows me her creation, saying, " I'm going to go put this in my book bag now."

Today the typical things happened for Lauren during sign-up, and, as usual, she came to me to find out what she had signed up for. She began playing with little blocks and dinosaur figures, a new choice for her, and she played for about ten minutes. Then she came to see me. "Penny, I am kind of lonesome doing this." I expressed concern and asked aloud if anyone would like to play with Lauren. There were several volunteers. Jennifer, another first-year student had been happily working on a book for me; instead, she nicely switched her choice to play with Lauren. She drifted back to her book once or twice, however.

I was pleased that Lauren expressed her feelings about being lonely. I wonder if she will consider seeking out choices where groups of students are already signed up, so that she will be assured of company. As she becomes more secure, Lauren will trust herself to read the choices and will trust other children to help her in this process. At any rate, it is interesting watching Lauren choosing what is right for her.

I share these stories to point out the importance of choice for people of all ages. Allowing people to choose ensures their freedom to develop; it creates risk takers. Both Phoebe and Lauren were making discoveries about themselves through the choices they were making. Their school settings provided them with varying degrees of support. In researching and writing *Choosing to Learn*, Jane and I made many discoveries, too. We became more and more convinced that choice should be the mainstay of our program. We discovered that our role as educators must be to provide the necessary security to our students to enable them to make appropriate choices. In the presence of choice, we saw all the various facets of our students' education falling into place. We looked to our students, to our families, to the experts, to our colleagues, to our students' parents, and within ourselves to explore choosing to learn in our multiage class.

In the first chapter, "The Option of Choice," Jane explores the rationale for student choice from the point of view of educators in the field and from our own perspectives as teachers who are "letting go" and encouraging students to take ownership of their learning. I focus on our students in the second and third chapters. In Chapter 2, "Choice Time," I describe the varied activities that occur during the daily Choice Time in our classrooms and explore the reasons why it has become our most valued part of the day. In Chapter 3, "Making Choices in School," I show how we give our students opportunities throughout the day to make many choices that impact their learning.

In Chapter 4, "The Teacher's Role," Jane describes the unique role of the teacher in a classroom where students are encouraged to be in charge of their own learning. In the fifth chapter, "Envisioning Curriculum," I show how our students have an important voice in directing our course of study. I describe the progression of our recent space theme from beginning to end, detailing opportunities for student choice and input.

Jane describes how parents help their children learn to make choices and become engaged in their learning in Chapter 6, "The Parents' Role." In Chapter 7, "The Responsibility of Choice," she describes how students become committed to their education. In the final chapter, "Looking at the Learner," I portray two of our students, showing how they progressed as learners in our classroom.

Jane and I are in a quandary lately, as our role as educators continues to shift. What should we call ourselves? The label *teacher* doesn't seem to fit. We will keep thinking about it as we keep working at making school a better place to be. Perhaps someday, as the ideal school we envision comes closer to reality, students and teachers, young and old, will truly choose to be learners together.

Acknowledgments

We thank all the members of our multiage family, the children and their parents, whose interactions have given us so many rich stories to tell. We also thank them for their caring support and for their valuable contributions to this work.

We thank our husbands for their support of our work. We especially thank them for cooking meals, for cleaning house, and for all the other ways, small and large, that they made life easier for us while we were writing this book.

The Option of Choice   *1*

Jane Doan

It is not every day that you can pick up the Sunday comics and find your educational philosophy printed there, but it happened to me.

One Sunday my husband Bob made the early morning run to the local store for the newspapers. With our breakfasts in one hand and the papers in the other we adjourned to the screened-in porch overlooking our yard. As usual, I grabbed first for the *Boston Globe* and went straight to the comics section. I pulled it out and sat back to read "Calvin and Hobbes," my favorite. This particular cartoon proved remarkable. In it Hobbes points out a snake skimming across the ground. He and Calvin then ask each other many questions, finally realizing that they know very little about snakes. Hobbes suggests that perhaps Calvin's mom would get them a book to find out more. They excitedly begin to run to the house, commenting that they will become experts. Suddenly Calvin realizes that he is on vacation, and he doesn't want to learn anything. Hobbes responds, "If nobody makes you do it, it counts as fun." The last frame of the cartoon shows Calvin and Hobbes lying on the grass looking at a book. They are both sighing, "Coooooolll" (Watterson 1995).

As I finished reading and chuckling, I found myself thinking how this cartoon related to what Penny and I are trying to achieve in our multiage classroom. What Hobbes knows instinctively has taken us many years to incorporate into our program. Children learn when they want to learn. When they feel ownership and control of their learning, not only will they enjoy that learning, but they will challenge themselves to ever higher learning. We have tried in our multiage program to offer children the opportunity to be free to learn. We try not to "make them" do it. Instead, we allow children to discover that learning is fun!

Allowing children the option of choice in their learning is not easy for us. There are times when we find ourselves reverting to controlling the children, their behavior, their socializing, and their learning. At times, Penny and I look at what we are doing in dismay as we realize that we have once again missed an opportunity to allow the children ownership of their learning or their behavior. Other times we are not sure that the ownership we allow the children is truly leading to self-disciplined, responsible behavior. Fortunately, the children in our multiage program manage to show us that they *are* capable of becoming responsible, autonomous people, perhaps even in spite of us.

An occurrence at one of our pumpkin weeding parties one summer provides a good example of our confusion in our struggle to encourage autonomy in our students. For the past several years we have been planting, caring for, harvesting, and marketing pumpkins as a class/family project. Planting, harvesting, and marketing take place during the school year as a class activity. Taking care of the plants occurs during the summer, when children and their families come together at Penny's farm to thin and weed our crop.

One day early in July parents and children began arriving at Penny's farm about 5:20 P.M. We socialized for a while, waiting for more "weeders" to arrive. Several children gathered in Penny's large yard to play catch. A few children sat on the grass talking together. Others stayed close to their parents, and one very tired student, Amanda, slept in her mom's car. Penny and I chatted with the parents, catching up on the news of their families' summer experiences.

After a little while, Penny called everyone together at the far end of the pumpkin patch and began discussing our crop. The plants had grown significantly since the last weeding event, and Penny wished to make sure that the children noticed not only the change in the size of the plants, but also how each individual variety was doing. She had just begun to discuss the black plastic experiment to keep down the weeds when another car turned into the driveway. Through the car's open windows we could hear William talking quite boisterously with his friend Charles. They had arrived! William ran from the parking area to join us, talking loudly all the way. When he joined the group he seemed not to notice that Penny was talking. He noisily greeted several children and started a discussion with one of them. He was making sure that this weeding party was going to move to his agenda.

William's behavior surprised us. He seemed to have forgotten the one rule of our multiage family: "To treat others as you would like to be treated." William always expected that others would listen to him. Would he notice that Penny was talking and begin to listen to her? We watched as Charles whispered to William. William looked around, smiled impishly, and quieted down.

Penny continued to point out that weeds had not grown between the two rows where we had spread black plastic over the ground. She asked why there were no weeds, and several children, including William, gave their ideas. After sharing several viewpoints, we agreed that the weeds there had not been able to get any sun, so they couldn't grow.

Penny then questioned whether we should take up the black plastic now. She explained that we did not know if plastic was a good surface for pumpkins to rest on as they grew. She proposed an experiment of keeping the plastic where it was to help with weed control. Several parents expressed their views. It seemed that some people felt strongly that it was worth taking a chance with the plastic. They reminded us of how tall the weeds had been at harvest time last year. They talked of the difficulty of walking through those weeds to find the pumpkins. Others were just as strong in their conviction that the pumpkins would rot if they sat on the plastic with water puddles under them. The discussion went on. We could not come to consensus.

William raised his hand. "Why don't we vote on it?" he asked reasonably. Everyone seemed satisfied by this suggestion. We voted to leave the plastic on the ground. Everyone was happy that the problem had been solved in a democratic way. The work of the weeding party began. Later, we had our picnic suppers, played and talked together, and then the children and their families headed home.

After the weeders left, Penny and I talked about the experience. We had been annoyed with William when he arrived. Initially, his behavior had been thoughtless. It had taken Charles's reminder to get him ready to be a part of the group. Later, though, William suggested that we vote to solve our quandary about the plastic. He was thinking, problem solving, being a responsible contributor to the group. In talking about William we realized that he is developing into an autonomous person. He is able to think for himself. In his worldview, he does distinguish between right and wrong. When Charles pointed out to him what was going on, he did change his behavior. It was his initial behavior that had irked us. Yet William's expectation that the weeding party was a time for visiting and doing, certainly one of our goals for having this get-together, led him to arrive in a most talkative mode. His choice to chat with his friends was based on his previous weeding party experiences. If he had been among the early arrivals he would have already had his socializing time, and he would have immediately understood that this was a discussion time.

Our negative reaction to his early behavior was a response once again to our need to be "in control." We thought William was being rude. He had taken us by surprise, barging in like he was the only person on earth when everyone else was listening carefully to Penny's talk. It occurred to us that we had never before tried to conduct a formal lesson at any of the pumpkin weeding parties. We had forgotten momentarily that this evening's activity was the children's choice. We had forgotten that if this weeding party was to be successful, the children had to be responsible and take ownership for their roles in the pumpkin project. We had to allow them the option of making this choice. William and Charles helped us get back on track, to realize that this real work of pumpkin farming was the children's choice. We were not making them do it. It could count for fun.

Our confusion and thoughts about just how to encourage student ownership and responsibility in the classroom have led to the writing of this book. We truly do not want to *make* children learn. We know that children must be responsible for their own learning. We believe that they must be the ones to "own" that learning.

We are not alone in our belief that children can take charge of their educational lives, that they are capable of making choices and taking responsibility for those choices. Constance Kamii wrote about student decision making more than ten years ago. She discusses why opportunities for student autonomy must start early and how this can be achieved. "The autonomy of five year olds does not happen by chance. It is the result of exchanging viewpoints with other children and adults day in and day out, and of being allowed to make decisions. . . . we must reduce our adult power . . . and let them make decisions for themselves (Kamii 1984, 13, 14).

Since we began coteaching in 1988, Penny and I have worked at doing just that. We constantly look at what we are doing in the classroom and try to find ways to give our students more power over their school day. Our Choice Time has evolved from a twenty-minute period two days a week to a full half hour each day. The Choice activities are often student suggested and student led. Our teacher-directed reading and writing conferences have changed into literacy goal-setting conferences in which the students decide on the ways in which they will work toward becoming better readers and writers. We have instituted a Math Workshop one day a week in which children choose the math activity that best fits their current needs. Our Talking Journal Time is no longer teacher led, but is run by the children. The children have direct input into developing our curriculum. They decide the questions we will concentrate on, give suggestions for the activities we will do, and bring in their parents and other relatives as guest experts. The children are responsible for deciding which room to work in, where to sit, what snack to eat, what books to read, and what topics to write about. We have worked hard to be able to see the many ways in which children can take responsibility for themselves and their learning in our classrooms. We know full well that these changes are only the beginning. As Penny says, "Once you begin to give the children ownership, you see more and more ways in which they can be in charge."

Penny and I have been teaching since the early 1970s. Some of our early teaching experiences were in multiage (combined) classes. We have always worked to have a child-centered curriculum, but changing from being the directors of what happens in our classrooms to allowing children to take responsibility and ownership for their learning has been a long trip for us. In looking back at how we have changed as teachers over the years, we feel that Tomm J. Elliott's assessment of his work in the classroom could have been said by both of us. "I must be slow, but it took me awhile to figure out that the more I took myself out of the process, the more the students assumed ownership of it" (Elliott 1993, 30). For the past six years we have been consciously working to take ourselves out of the process of being responsible for children's learning. We want that responsibility to be theirs.

I began my teaching career weighted down with four years of "teaching of . . ." college courses, with a teacher's manual for every subject. These courses had convinced me that there was a perfect method of teaching and that it was to be found in the manuals. I was taught to believe that the experts who wrote and published those books knew best what my students needed. Consequently, I did believe in them, and the publishers of the manuals and my principal were quick to reinforce that belief.

In the 1970s I became influenced by the writings of John Holt, Jonathan Kozol, and George Dennison. With the help of these authors I came to see that there was a lot more to educating children than just following teacher manuals. I began to work as hard at getting to know my students as I worked at unlearning the manuals. I began to understand that teaching involves the whole child, not just her intellect. But my role as a teacher, while more sympathetic to the children, was still that of the person in charge. I continued to be a dispenser of information. I was still "the teacher"—a person with no personal history, just lots of power.

In the 1980s I was introduced to the writings of Nancie Atwell, Frank Smith, Jane Hansen, Lucy Calkins, Donald Graves, and Don Murray. These authors promoted student ownership of their reading and writing. They encouraged me to allow children to make decisions about their literacy growth on their own or with minimal teacher direction. I tried some of their ideas and was enthusiastic about the results. I observed in Penny's classroom and saw how she encouraged her students to take ownership of their learning. I was impressed with how thoughtful her students were about their work, and I went back to my classroom convinced that the best change I could make in my teaching was to give over some of my "power" to the children.

Penny had come to teaching with quite a different background from mine. She had graduated from college with a B.A. in English literature. Then she moved to Maine and got a teaching job. Only then did she begin to take education courses, and she was fortunate in her professors. In her first course on teaching reading and language arts, her professor supported individualized instruction and encouraged the teachers, not teachers' manuals, to be in charge of each student's curriculum. A math course she audited at the University of Maine promoted the discovery method of learning, allowing children to make choices. She was reading some of the same authors I was reading, and she had also discovered the writings of Caroline Pratt, Sylvia Ashton Warner, and A. S. Neill.

Penny began her teaching career in Fairfield, Maine, when that school district was still committed to the use of basal readers. A friend was working as a reading specialist in the neighboring town of Waterville. She told Penny about their individualized reading program and encouraged her to apply there. Penny began teaching at the South Grammar School in Waterville in 1970. A few years later I joined her there. During our four years at South Grammar, the entire staff of this K–4 school experimented both with the multiage concept and with student choice. We discovered many benefits of allowing our students to choose activities or areas of study. We found that our children were more excited about their learning when they felt they had a say in what they were going to do. We became friends through our work in this innovative school. We continued to read texts on education and to share the books we found. Our experiences there led to our coteaching in a multiage class many years later.

After several years, I moved on to a private school and Penny moved to small rural school in Albion, Maine. Independently, we continued to question our teaching practices and to move toward offering the children in our classrooms more and more opportunities to take ownership of their learning.

Some years later, Penny and I began to take graduate degree courses together at the University of Maine, and during our two-and-a-half-hour round-trip ride from our homes to Orono we carried on lengthy conversations about education. The result of these talks was our decision to coteach in a primary multiage classroom. We began working together in 1988. Through coteaching, our school lives became dominated by the question of what was best for the children. We regularly looked at what was happening in our classrooms and asked ourselves why we were doing it. If we could not truly answer that it was good for the children, we rethought that idea and moved toward what could be better. Our coteaching has been marked by what I consider positive growth as educators. Working together, we have been able to *reflect*.

These reflections led to our coauthoring *Full Circle: A New Look at Multiage Education*. In writing that book we looked very closely at our educational philosophy as it related to multiage education. Even before the book was finished we knew that we wanted to look more closely at why we believed in student responsibility and ownership in the classroom. We wanted to examine just what we were doing to promote student autonomy. During the writing of *Full Circle*, the idea of choice kept popping up. Sometimes, we questioned whether the thesis of the book was about the multiage concept or about student ownership. We knew we needed to write another book in order to give the idea of student ownership and responsibility the exposure it deserves. This book, then, is the result of that need and of our reflecting on what our students, their parents, and we, their teachers, do to promote student autonomy.

Choice

In our multiage program we now offer the children many choices throughout the day. The children are given opportunities to self-direct their own learning, as well as to help direct the actions the entire class will take. At these times, Penny and I try to become "just another vote," with that vote having the same weight as each child's vote. We work at moving away from dictating all that will happen in our classrooms. We believe, as Constance Kamii states, "Children learn to make wise decisions not by being obedient, but by making choices and decisions for themselves" (Kamii 1984, 13).

We work hard to provide opportunities for student choice. Some of the choices the children make are fairly simple. Others are more complex and more directly impact their learning.

One small choice we offer our children is whether to come directly to our classrooms or to go out onto the playground when they get off the buses in the morning. Every day each child makes the choice that best fits her needs. One child may need to stay on the playground to spend more time with an older sibling or to play with friends who are in other classrooms. Another child may come running into the classroom to share with us a special occurrence in her life or to be sure she is able to sign up for a Choice Time activity she has wanted to do. Each child begins the school day in an autonomous manner, being in control of where to go and what to do once she is there.

"Hi, Jane." Nancy smiles as she enters the classroom. "Are there any Post-its I can put into the class record book?"

"Right here," I respond, passing her the pile of yellow Post-its, yesterday's observations during message time.

Nancy arrives early to our room every day with the hope of being able to do some job to help me. She is a quiet, unassertive child in a large group, and the smaller group, before school time, gives her the opportunity to feel comfortable asking and doing.

Tom arrives with his mother in tow. He likes to use before-school time to share with his mom the contents of his cubby—all the work he has done for the last week resides there.

Alice follows Tom into the room, yells a "Hi, Jane," signs up for clay, and runs to the paper shelf. Soon she is writing her mom a letter. Because of her parents' divorce, separating from her mom to come to school has been difficult for her. Her daily letters are a way for her to keep that special connection.

Denice arrives and joins her best friend Tom. She has work she wants Tom's mom to see, too.

The twenty minutes before the bell rings pass quickly. As the children have slowly arrived, I have had the opportunity to greet each one, and they have had the opportunity to choose to be in the room and to decide what they wish to do at this time. Through the option of this small choice, the stage has been set for the children. They already know that school is a place where they will make decisions for themselves, where they will have opportunities to direct their learning.

In our multiage program, we strive to treat the children as we would like to be treated. Both Penny and I work best in situations where we feel that we have a choice. We do not work well in situations where what we are to do is dictated by others. We believe this to be true of all people, old and young. The area of literacy education has supported this idea for years. "Given the choice between having a choice and being told what to do, most adults will always opt for the option. Kids will, too" (Kassens 1984, 48).

The children spend their day making the small and larger choices needed to direct their learning. They take pride in being able to make decisions for themselves. They become confident and self-assured. We see the pleasure they take in their work.

It is our belief that when children share in decision making they have a more positive attitude toward school. We believe that an element of choice helps to create a more positive feeling in the class. Other teacher-researchers agree with us. Moira Proudfoot discovered that the element of choice helped to create a positive feeling in her math class (Proudfoot 1992, 131). We believe that it is necessary for children to have opportunities for choice if they are to learn to lead autonomous lives.

Autonomy/Democracy

The importance of autonomy was pointed out to me by my own children. My daughter Kathryn went to college for her own reasons. She wanted to go and she planned to earn a degree in East Asian studies. She graduated from college with honors four years later, proud that she had accomplished *her* goal. My son Michael had a very different experience. He had no motivation toward the goal of attaining a college degree. He went to college because it was expected of him. His father and I gave him no other choice. He experimented in the areas of communication, business, and education. He looked to these as possible careers because of his parents' suggestions that they might be areas where he could succeed. But he found it impossible to earn a degree simply because others thought he should. So he left school. A few years later he discovered that he had a real passion for marine biology. He began college again—this time as his choice, for his purposes. And this time he was successful. He, too, graduated with honors.

Creating autonomous individuals must become the goal of educators and families. The world needs people who can think for themselves. We need people who do not blindly follow others. Members of a democracy must be able to think for themselves in order to govern themselves. When only one person in a classroom has the power to effect decisions, the students are being prepared to accept that others will make all decisions for them. When all the members of a classroom join together in making decisions, those members will come to understand how a democracy works.

Changing our classrooms into places where promoting autonomy is one of the guiding philosophies is not easy. Kamii writes: "Autonomy as the aim of education implies the need to rethink everything we do in the name of education. I do not have anything against 'good' behavior, 'right' answers, or the three R's. I am, in fact, all for them. But there is an enormous difference between a correct answer autonomously produced with personal conviction and one produced heteronomously by obedience. There is likewise an enormous difference between 'good' behavior autonomously chosen and 'good' behavior practiced through blind conformity" (Kamii 1982, 7).

One way to provide opportunities for the children to develop personal convictions is to allow them to make some of the classroom decisions that we had previously considered to be solely within the realm of the teacher. We no longer dictate a list of rules and consequences to govern the children and expect obedience to our ideas of proper behavior. We have given ownership of their behavior to them.

One year we asked the children early on, "What kind of community do you want our classroom to be?" The idea for this question came directly from a write-up of an interview between Alfie Kohn and Ron Brandt in the September 1995 issue of *Educational Leadership*. Penny and I both have been strongly influenced by Kohn's writings. His book *Punished by Rewards* had supported the decision we made years ago not to use gold stars or other incentive plans as ways to "motivate" learning.

The *Educational Leadership* article once again supported our beliefs on the issue of rewards, grades, and competition. Even more important, it pointed out to me that while I had been giving lip service to the idea of student ownership and responsibility, I still had a long way to go. In the article Kohn pointed out the difference between the questions "What do they want me to do and what will happen to me if I don't?" or "What do they want me to do and what will I get for doing it?" and the questions "What kind of person do I want to be?" or "What kind of classroom do I want to have?" (Brandt 1995, 16).

I knew that I wanted to be asking the latter questions in our classroom. Holding a discussion on what kind of community the children wanted was a good place for me to start.

"What is a community?" was the question I asked the day after I read the interview. Several children wanted to offer an answer.

William stated, "It's a place where you go and do stuff."

Doug tried, "A community is a place where people work together."

Joanna said, "It's where people work."

"What does it say in the dictionary?" asked Charles.

The class dictionary provided a good generic definition: "a group of people living in the same area or under the same government." We all agreed on this definition. The next step was to decide if our classroom was indeed a community. We were all in agreement that we did live a good part of our lives together here, and therefore we were a community. We progressed on to the original question: What kind of a community did we want? Susan requested a community where people take care of one another. Doug wanted it to be a place where people help each other with their work. Fred thought it should be a place where everyone felt okay, comfortable with everything. Joanna thought that it was important to live where people help each other learn. Alice agreed, adding that it should be a place where people show each other how to do things. William insisted that he wanted our community to be a place where people communicate.

The discussion went on until recess time. We decided this was too important for a one-day time frame and scheduled further talks the next week. In the meantime the children were asked to think about it at home and write or draw their ideas about what makes a good community on their homework papers.

The following Monday we went over the ideas about what kind of community we wanted which the children had placed on the backs of their homework. Allison suggested that in our community people should care about others' work. Her picture showed a child walking carefully past another student's work, which was on the floor. Britt suggested that people in our community should not be sloppy. They should clean up their messes. Eddie thought it was important to have a community where people were respectful of others by being quiet at work times.

This day's discussion was as exciting as the previous one. The children knew what kind of a community they wanted and they had offered suggestions on how they could work toward having the caring, supportive, respectful community they desired. Penny and I recently looked back over the months that have passed since these discussions. We agreed that the children are making sure that they have the kind of community they want through their actions. They have taken the responsibility for their roles as community members, and they are doing this by choosing to behave autonomously.

Rethinking what we do as educators in terms of promoting student autonomy has been an important aspect of our research during the six years we have worked together in our multiage setting. During these years we have gradually found more and more areas in which the children can make important decisions that affect their education. From choosing their activities at Choice Time to having ownership over their behavior, the children in our multiage program share in the responsibility of managing our classrooms. We have changed these classrooms from autocracies to democracies.

We believe that the choices children are encouraged to make in our classroom lead to the development of autonomy. The children discuss their choices with each other and with their parents and teachers. They share their ideas freely, feeling confident that their words are of value to their peers. They understand that "Why?" is an essential question in decision making. They come to make decisions confidently. This talk is valued by teachers, parents, and the children, and it is invaluable in developing the children's sense of autonomy. Kamii states: "The most important elements for children's development of autonomy are opportunities to exchange viewpoints with other people and the possibility of making decisions" (Kamii 1984, 12–13).

"What is your choice today?" Missy asks Alice.

"Writing and Drawing," says Alice.

"Why did you choose that?" queries Missy.

"I am going to write a letter to every one of my friends. And I am going to decorate an envelope for each one. And then I will put them in my friends' cubbies as a surprise. What are you going to choose?"

"Reading with a Friend."

"Why?"

"I brought my favorite book to school and I want to share it with someone."

Children in our program know that they have control over many of their school activities. While they know that their ideas and choices are valued by all of us, they know that they are responsible for their choices and decisions. They also know that Penny and I are there to help them with their decision making.

The children know that we respect their decisions and they respect our efforts to nudge them in one direction or another. It is this mutual respect which is at the heart of our student choice program. Kamii again supports our educational theory: "A child who feels respected today is more likely to accept a suggestion tomorrow than one who feels he was forced to submit to adult power" (Kamii 1982, 8).

In our multiage program we make every effort to help children view school as an environment where it is safe to problem-solve and make choices. We try to support the children as decision makers and to let them know that our support will be there regardless of the outcome of their decision. "For children to develop in ways that will allow them to be self-determining, they need environments that support their initiations and allow them to make choices"(Deci and Chandler 1986, 590).

Student choice leads to motivated students. Children who have ownership and control of their learning will tend to be more inclined to continue learning. They will develop the self-esteem necessary to become independent learners. In discussing a study (Deci et al., 1981) of fourth-through sixth-grade classrooms, Deci states, "Children in classes of teachers who were oriented toward supporting autonomy became intrinsically motivated, perceived themselves to be more competent, and developed higher self-esteem than children in the classrooms of more controlling teachers"(Deci and Chandler 1986, 590).

One of the shyest children I have ever met was a member of our multiage class. For the first year she was with us, Nancy chose not to speak. She was quiet at Talking Journal, quiet at Morning Meeting, quiet at Choice Time and all the other times of the day. Nancy did not feel comfortable answering questions, even the simplest ones. She listened and she watched for over a full year. I believe that Nancy was noticing how everyone valued each child's contributions to our discussions. I believe she was looking for a time or a situation in which she would dare to contribute. Finally, in her second year in the program, she found it.

The class was discussing ways to spend our pumpkin earnings. The children had many suggestions.

"Let's all go to Disney World," exclaimed Doug, hoping we could visit his vision of paradise.

"I think we should all go to get our hair done. Then we would all look pretty," suggested Joanna.

"An ice cream party would be nice."

"How about a pizza party."

"Or we could order Chinese."

Nancy's hand went up. "We should spend the money on something that we all want. It should be something that would last a long time."

"I agree!" stated her friend Dani. "We don't want to waste the money on something that will be gone in a flash."

I was thrilled. Nancy was feeling safe in our group. It had been her decision to become a vocal participant in our class. She had taken the risk of sharing her viewpoint. I knew that she would continue to do so. She was on her way to becoming an autonomous person, confident of her ability to participate in group decisions.

Penny and I believe in a democratic classroom. We believe that for our national democracy to succeed, children must begin to understand democratic principles at very young ages. Our goals in teaching reflect that belief. We strive to make our program a place where democratic principles are practiced and valued by all. We try to follow a path similar to what Kathleen Long recommends: "If you want a democratic society, create space for students to practice democratic principles. If you want students who are responsible and self-controlled, create space for them to learn responsibility and self-control. If you want students who are creative and committed, allow them to share in the planning, implementation, and assessment of their own educational activities. If you want students that are caring and responsible, treat them in that manner. If you want students who reach beyond the boundaries and apparent differences that separate people, nations, and ideas, structure your pedagogy on those principles" (Long 1994, 546).

Recently, the parent of a former student came by to tell us of a conversation she had had with our principal. Keith, her son, and another former student are now in the advanced (5/6) multiage program at our school. They had gone to the principal with the idea of using student monitors to help keep the playground a safe environment. The two of them had read about a school in California where student monitors were working well, and they had written to that school for more information on their monitoring program. They took the results of their research to the principal and asked if this could be an option for our school. They said that they knew it might take time to get a student monitoring system in place, that it might not happen until they had left our school for junior high, but that they felt so strongly about it they wanted to have a role in getting the process going. The principal agreed to work with them on the idea. She praised them for their commitment to their school. Then she added that they must be feeling proud of themselves. Keith commented that he had received the best start possible in school because he had been in Penny and Jane's multiage class. "When you start out there, you learn to think and solve problems," he stated.

"Well," countered the principal, "you must have strong support from your parents."

"Oh yes!" exclaimed Keith. "Our parents are the best. But it was our start with Penny and Jane that helped us the most."

We were amazed. This parent's story made our day—our week—our year! Keith was putting into practice what we had been trying to offer him. He was seeing himself as an autonomous person, an individual capable of making positive changes in the world he lives in. He was able to discuss issues with adults on an equal level, and he was attributing his ability to do so to the experiences he had had in our multiage program. Maybe we were doing something right. Or maybe his parents really did have quite a lot to do with his sense of autonomy!

Children have the right to a fair and democratic form of education. All children have the right to be successful in school. All children have the right to an educational environment that encourages them to think for themselves, problem-solve, and take risks. Emma Holmes (1991, 176) makes great sense to us in her discussion of students' rights. "Children have the right to be taught well and to experience success. Furthermore, education in a democratic class atmosphere should imply that students have opportunities to participate in group life and to communicate with others. . . . Students' rights encompass being psychologically secure in school, that is, being respected, listened to, given some privacy, involved in appropriate levels of decision making, treated fairly, and taught by a caring supportive teacher" (Holmes 1991, 176).

It is these rights that we strive to protect in our program. The children have opportunities to decide where they will sit, what they will read or write, what activity they will do, what room they wish to be in, and which teacher they wish to work with. As they make these choices they realize that we see them as competent people, that we respect their decisions, that we value them as individuals, that we care for them.

Ownership/Responsibility

We agree with Anna Kelman's writings. In "Choices for Children," she states:

> Responsibility and choices are connected. I doubt you can have one without the other and therein lies a difficulty. Most of us would agree we want our children to grow up to be responsible adults; but, are we willing to allow them the experiences that lead to that outcome?
>
> Children need to be allowed many choices. If you don't learn to choose which clothes to wear or what to eat for breakfast on a given day, you might not develop a feeling of control. If you don't feel some control, you will have trouble feeling responsible. Making choices is a necessary step on the road to acquiring feelings of control. Only after

we take that step can we begin to take some responsibility for our behavior" (Kelman 1990, 42).

Kamii also echoes these thoughts. In 1984 she stated, "Children can become responsible only when they are truly responsible for the decisions they make. As long as decisions are made by someone else, children are not responsible for them because all they have to do is obey" (Kamii 1984, 13).

There is really not much we can add to these two powerful writings, except to tell what happened when we tried to give college students choices in their learning.

Several years ago Penny and I taught a course, Methods of Teaching Reading and Language Arts, at the University of Maine. We prepared our syllabus, leaving many of the assignments open-ended and offering the students the opportunity to decide for themselves what projects they would do. We hoped to give these students ownership over what they would be doing so they could help themselves to become competent reading and writing teachers. The questions we received were endless. They wanted to know how many pages should be in the projects, what topics to choose, what models to use, and so on. In short, they wanted us to tell them exactly what to do, in great detail. They were very frustrated by the idea that they were in charge of making these important decisions. In the past all of this kind of thinking had been done for them, and they resented us for not doing it for them now. I believe that they suspected that we had hidden criteria for grading the projects. They could not believe that what we wanted was for them to think about what would help them in their learning and then act on that understanding.

By midterm, the students began to trust us. The midterm exam consisted of individual conferences in which we asked the students to reflect on their learning so far and to think about what they felt they needed to know more about. We gave them the opportunity to help decide the direction of the rest of the semester. The idea that they were in charge of their own learning began to seem less foreign to them. Decisions about what they could do to increase their learning began to be made. The students began to be comfortable with making choices for themselves. They began to take responsibility for their learning.

We found it sad that these students had not had opportunities for choices earlier in their educational careers. It is our hope that children leaving our primary multiage class will continue to take responsibility for themselves, that they will continually ask themselves how they can help themselves become even better learners.

Choice Time

2

Penelle Chase

It was the first day back to school after our week-long February break. Children off the buses were filtering into the common area outside of our rooms, shedding their outdoor clothes and hanging them on the coat rack. As they came into the classroom they greeted me and each other. There was lots of easygoing talk; we were all glad to see each other. After the children stowed their personal belongings in their cubbies, many of them inspected and discussed the choices listed on the large dry board. Several children signed their names under a choice that attracted them. Others went to Jane's room to check out the choices on her board. A few students asked another child for help reading the choice offerings. In a primary multiage class where reading abilities vary widely, we help each other out. As children finished signing up, they began to gather on the low benches where we would soon begin our sharing time. Some children and I were already sitting there, talking together before school officially began.

I asked, "What's your favorite time of day in school? What have you missed most this last week? Now, don't say recess! Don't say lunch, either!"

Curtis piped up, and several children echoed him: "Choice Time!"

I questioned the children further. "Why do you like Choice Time best?"

The response was overwhelming: "Because we get to play!"

We talked a little more; I wondered if *all* the choices at Choice Time are *play*.

"Is Big Blocks play?" I asked.

"Yes, because you get to play with what you build after you build it."

"Is Constructions play?"

"Yes, because you get to make something you want out of junk."

"Is Reading/Writing/Drawing play?"

"Well, maybe not. Maybe that's work."

Together we looked at the Choice sign-up board and considered some of the other options. The children decided. Dress-ups are play. Penny's Math is not play. Listening Center is not play. Bricks are play. Goal Conferences are not play. Unfortunately, the bell rang then, and the Pledge of Allegiance via the intercom was imminent.

Though our discussion was cut short, I found that I had many more questions for the children. What constitutes *work* and what constitutes *play* in their minds? Can work be fun, and therefore be considered play? Do you learn by working or by playing, or both? What makes Choice Time good for you? Another time I would ask the children some of these questions to find out from them how Choice Time impacts their learning.

Some form of Choice Time has been a regularly scheduled part of our school day for several years now. When we instituted it, our primary multiage program was four years old and changing all the time. As teachers, we were happy with the workshop orientation of our day. Our Communications and Investigations workshops gave students opportunities to meet their needs as learners in an open-ended environment. But we noticed that many wonderful learnings were occurring during even less structured times. For instance, on days that we were forced by inclement weather to stay indoors for recess, we often allowed the children to decide on their own how they would spend the half-hour period. We were usually impressed by the wide range of activities that the students chose to do, their involvement in their choices, and the aura of calm productivity that pervaded the classrooms.

We also observed children creating learning opportunities for themselves at other unscheduled times. For example, many times after children completed workshop tasks, they spontaneously pursued activities on their own. Often we would look around at the close of a workshop period and like what we saw: children reading in pairs, kids writing or drawing together, or children playing games, singing, reciting poems, or talking together. Other times, students asked for time to pursue special interests: "It's my mom's birthday today. Can I make her a card?" "I brought this game I got. It's Yahtzee. Can I teach it to some kids today?" "I've been studying about Jupiter on my computer at home. Can I go to the library today to see if they have any books on Jupiter?" We were enthused when children initiated projects like these, and we tried to provide time to accommodate their pressing concerns. We knew that capitalizing on their excitement of the moment would result in learning. The problem always seemed to be that old bugaboo—time. As open as our schedule was, it was not always unencumbered enough to allow students the freedom to pursue these immediate interests.

We realized that we yearned for an unstructured block of time so that students could pursue their interests on a daily basis. We had another concern, too. The children in our classes ranged in age from five to eight years. They were at all levels of development. We were feeling good about the ways in which we were addressing the children's academic requirements, but we weren't so sure we were fulfilling their physical, social, and emotional needs. We were aware that many of our students needed more unstructured time to move, talk, and play. A scheduled free time was long overdue in our program.

Midyear we initiated our first Choice Time. As free time was an unheard of commodity in this era of "time on task" and teaching to specific goals and objectives, we began tentatively. We instituted a twenty-minute Choice Time at the end of the day, two days a week. We told the children that this was a time when they could do what they chose. It would be like inside recess; they could play games, draw, read, write, play with blocks, use the dress-ups, or whatever other activity they liked. As we expected, the children embraced the idea eagerly. Unfortunately, that initial experiment with Choice Time was disappointing. It was too open-ended. Some children found it difficult to decide what to do with so few parameters to guide them. It was too short. Many children had just begun their activity when it was time to clean up. And, it was at the wrong time of day. At the end of the day children were mentally making the school-to-home transition; they seemed to have trouble directing themselves. For some, whatever energy they had left after a long day at school manifested itself in whining and bickering. This collective fussiness and the fact that we had not trained the children in Choice Time procedures and behavior caused us to wonder why we had ever come up with this idea in the first place.

Luckily, there were a few good things going on that saved Choice Time. Children were having opportunities to talk and play with each other. The birthday cards were getting written, some independent research was going on, the games and puzzles were coming off the shelves. These bright spots kept us committed to the concept of a block of time for student choice, and we continued to tinker with the format of Choice Time over the next few years. It's gotten better: Choice Time in our classrooms now offers children opportunities to make decisions, to work on relationships, and to learn on their own. Each day the children choose from the eight to twelve offerings listed on the Choices board in each of our classrooms. They may go to either Jane's or Penny's room to sign up. Choice Time occurs mid-morning, between two sit-and-listen times. Some of the choices like Big Blocks and Bricks are standard offerings and appear on the list each day. Other choices may be connected to a theme we are exploring, like adding to the Space Bulletin Board or working on the Dinosaur Puzzle. Still other choices may have been suggested by the children, like "Help Rebecca Make Her Schoolbook." Others may rise from an actual need of the classroom, like "Straighten the Game Shelves." Some of the choices are dictated by our parent volunteers' schedules. One day "Cooking with Sandra" may be up. Another day Workbench is listed, because a parent helper is expected.

Each of the choices has numbered spaces below it, indicating how many people may sign up for that choice. Once every two or three weeks children are signed up by Jane and me for a Goals Conference. On the day of the Goals Conference, the child will work on literacy goals with the teacher during Choice Time. This format for managing Choice Time gives the children some direction. However, the choices within the structure are fairly open-ended. The time is designed so that students can work and play independently. Because we spend several weeks early in the year helping children to develop this independence, Choice Time practically runs itself. Usually, it is the most mellow time of our day. Presently, the period is thirty minutes long, and we are considering making it longer or adding another Choice Time into our daily schedule.

The following journal entry describes Choice Time the day after our February break, the same day that the children and I talked together about their favorite time in school. This portrayal of a typical Choice Time session in our classroom may illustrate why we have come to value this time as highly as our students do.

Penny's Day Book   February 26

Since it's the first day back after vacation I did not schedule any Goals Conferences today. This free time for me is truly a luxury, as I was able to observe the children and take some notes during Choice Time. I think that I will keep a record for awhile of the choices the children pick. I noticed some interesting things today. Bradley was the only child from Jane's room who signed up for a choice in my room. And Heidi and Carrie were the only ones from my room who signed up in Jane's room. I was surprised that so few children left their home rooms for Choice Time. Maybe they stayed close because it was the first day back from vacation. It would be interesting to keep track of who goes where for Choice Time. I am envisioning a sheet with kids' names down the side, ruled off in boxes, with a week's dates across the top. We could fill in what each child did for a choice that day, and in which room. Just for curiosity's sake.

The choices listed on my board today were *Big Blocks; Reading/ Writing/Drawing; Bricks; Legos; Playhouse; Painting; Game (You Choose); Clean Cubby; Constructions; Clean Up Little Room; Penny's Math.* Here's what the children who signed up in my room were doing.

Ronnie did Legos by himself. His sidekick, Bryant, had already signed up for Bricks with Lauren. Since Bricks was filled up, Ronnie had to choose something else. He tried to convince Bryant to forsake Bricks and do something with him, but to no avail! Ronnie was okay; he seemed to be having a good time playing with Legos on his own.

Five children had signed up for Reading/Writing/Drawing. All five of the children were drawing, but each of their drawings had some writing on it. Erin, Cindy, and Rebecca sat at a table together, using markers. Erin made a big poster/letter for Rebecca. Jennifer made a big poster/birthday card for Cassie (we had found out at message time that it was Cassie's birthday—usually Jennifer has little to do with Cassie). Rebecca made a big poster with a message for her mom, "I love you Mom." Matthew worked by himself at another table. I didn't see what he was doing, but I asked him about it later. He was working on a map of where his clubhouse is going to be at home—he made it for Thomas. Serene had brought a packet of mouse stationery from home that she had gotten for a present. She worked on a thank-you letter to her Aunt Debbie. She brought her dictionary to me for help spelling "Debbie." I was interested that all the children were writing, as well as drawing, and that there were several connections between home and school in their projects.

Erica, Jamie, and Thomas cleaned out cubbies. Thomas had saved this task since before vacation—he had reminded me to write *Clean Cubby* up on the board for a choice this morning before school. Jamie had cleaned out her cubby several days before vacation, but she wanted to do it again, probably because Erica was doing it. And Erica most likely was intrigued by the idea of washing out her empty cubby, as she had seen Kyla do recently. Erica did load up a bag full of papers to take home, which immensely improved the state of her cubby. And Thomas was excited to find several pencils and other objects that didn't belong in his cubby.

Karen signed up for Clean Up Little Room, which we had turned into an art studio to go along with our previous theme. She loved that chore—taking down the pictures, sorting supplies, scrubbing paint off the easels and the table, sweeping the floor. The Little Room still looks like a wreck, but maybe more kids will sign up to help clean tomorrow. Several children were taking note of the good time Karen was having. We need to get the studio cleaned up, as we will begin our *Charlotte's Web* theme today, and soon we will decide what the Little Room will become next.

Constructions is always filled up. Three kids had the laundry basket of recyclable junk in the middle of the floor and were happily constructing. Andy made a double-hulled boat out of some odd plastic containers to use with his action figures at home. He was excited to show it to me and explain how it worked. Various-sized cardboard tubes came in handy. Gordon made handcuffs which he tried out on Curtis. (He will use them at home to handcuff his brother.) Curtis made binoculars. (He also says he will share them with his brother at home.) Again, I was interested that so many of the children connected their activity at school with plans for home.

Bryant and Kyla worked with Tricia, our sixth-grade helper, at Bricks. Mostly, Tricia constructed a huge tower out of the cardboard blocks. She stood on a chair to make it higher and higher. The other two children were content to hand her bricks and to watch. She put a little Lego man on the very top. The children wanted me to take a picture of it, but my camera was not at school. Bryant suggested that they draw a picture of it—he made two (and he included the little man safe on top, with another man falling). I was interested that he wanted a record of the tower. I challenged the kids to disassemble the tower without it falling down. They did, taking sections down at a time and handing them to a lower-down kid to put away. Tricia began a picture of the tower after it was down and invited the other children to add to it. I was interested that the younger kids followed her lead and willingly let her manage the play. Tricia and Bryant taped their pictures up on the wall, and Tricia assured the children that she would come back soon to help them build another even bigger tower.

Colby, Shannon, and Jody played an elaborate make-believe game of Aladdin with the big wooden blocks. They created a massive castle in the bench area. They were doing a lot of talking, some of it Aladdin-related and some of it about their vacation experiences.

Heidi brought a huge plastic van to school today, full of six assorted Barbie and Ken dolls. She told about it at Talking Journal—very briefly. I guess she felt it spoke for itself. Heidi went off to Jane's room, and I noticed the van at Choice Time on the big pillow by the kneeling table with a sign next to it—"Do Not Tuch—Thank you." As far as I know, no one did!

When I gave the children the five-minute warning, there were a few groans. Several children hurried to the snack table to get their snacks, which they had forgotten. I had to chivvy the children a bit to get them going at cleanup time. When we gathered at the benches before going to Jane's room for Investigations, I reminded them that we all need to pitch in and help each other when it's time to clean up.

All in all, it was a good, relaxing Choice Time. I do think it would be interesting to keep track for a while of the choices the children make. Why do they choose what they do?

We have Choice Time every day. Sometimes special events occur that require us to cut something out of our day. We always find a way to rearrange our schedule so that we can include Choice Time. Choice Time has gained this degree of importance in our program for many reasons. Above all, it is the children's favorite time of day, and that fact alone makes it valuable. Children who are in a rich learning environment and are happy cannot help but learn. Since learning is a high-priority goal in our multiage class, we are gratified to see many kinds of learning occurring as the children work and play during Choice Time. We see children becoming independent thinkers who can make decisions for themselves. We see children extending what they are learning at school to things that they are learning outside of school, and vice versa. We see children working on social relationships and developing skills in collaborating. We see children acquiring academic knowledge across all areas of the curriculum. We see children discovering how to value their learning through the choices that they make. Examples of children engaged in these various learnings will illustrate why it is not surprising that we look for ways to make our Choice Time period even longer.

Children Becoming Independent Thinkers

When we first began having a regularly scheduled Choice Time, we noticed that some children seemed to stick to the same choices day after day. Though we weren't officially keeping track, a few children were making a strong impression on us. Seven-year-old Jackson always chose to build with blocks and jealously attempted to keep a choice selection of them for his own use. Shawn, a first-year student, always chose Reading/Writing/Drawing, which manifested itself into a creation that involved using the stapler and many staples. One of our oldest children, Heidi, got someone to play Chutes and Ladders or Candyland with her every day. We worried about the narrowness of some of the other children's choices, too. One morning I said to Jane, "If Shawn staples another day, I will go nuts. Do you think I should tell him 'No stapling!' today? Should I make him try some other choice?"

Jane answered, "Let's be patient awhile longer. If it's Choice Time, we have to let the kids *choose.*"

"I know, but stapling every day can't be helping him that much."

"You never know!" Jane laughed. "Maybe it's doing wonders for his fine motor coordination. I understand your frustration, though. I see kids doing the same things every day, and I know that if they would just try some of the other choices, they would like them."

"Maybe we should do a Morning Message about trying new choices," I suggested.

"Good idea," Jane agreed. "Then we can have some of the kids talk about the things they are doing at Choice Time and maybe open the children's eyes to some of the possibilities."

Later that week we did the choice message, children told about their choices, and nothing changed. Not right away, at least. We toyed with the idea of devising some system that required children to vary their choices. Luckily, we had the sense not to intervene. We were determined to trust the children as learners. And slowly, we began to see children branching out into different directions in their choices. One day

Shawn abandoned the stapler and got involved with magic markers. For days, he covered large sheets of poster paper with random letters, messages to his Auntie Sue who was wintering in Florida. Jackson began creating maps to go with his block structures, and he began working more collaboratively with other children to build them. Heidi slowly began trying a wide range of other choices. For reasons that we can only guess at, these children decided to become involved in different activities. And they decided for themselves. They moved on to new challenges when they felt ready to do so.

We have learned that children experiment more freely when they thoroughly understand the activities. We have learned to ease into Choice Time slowly. At the beginning of the year we conscientiously explain a few choices at a time to the children. We show where supplies are kept, demonstrate how to use materials, and model cleaning up and putting things away. We rotate the children through the choices round-robin style in multiaged groups. Our returning older children help to acquaint the new students with the choice possibilities. After this orientation period, which takes several weeks, children are allowed to sign up for choices on their own.

Children continue to approach Choice Time in different ways in our classrooms. Some of them try a bit of everything, and some stick with the same choice for extended periods of time. But we have become secure in our belief that children develop uniquely, and that they can be in charge of at least some of that development. By respecting their choices at Choice Time, we show children that we value them as learners and that we trust them to make good decisions for themselves. Choice Time gives students the time and opportunity to become independent in their thinking.

Ironically, schools rarely provide occasions for inquiry. We have discovered that the free atmosphere of Choice Time promotes inquiry. Recently, I watched Kyla at Choice Time. She had signed up for Sta-blox, which are brightly colored wooden blocks hooked together internally with elastic bands. The family of one of our students had given the class several of these block strips as a present, and Kyla was fascinated by them. She sat by herself and played with them for fifteen minutes or so, twisting and turning the blocks to make various configurations. When I came over, she showed me what she was doing. "I'm confused," she confessed. "I thought that all these strips were the same size, but when I try to make two things out of them that look alike I can't do it."

"Hmmm," I said, and I sat down on the bench next to her, keeping an eye both on her and on the children working with blocks in the same area. I saw the problem. The strips were the same length when stretched out in a line. However, each block was longer than it was wide, so the way the blocks were turned changed the size of the resulting configuration. It took her awhile, but she persisted in playing with the blocks until she proved to herself that the strips were indeed the same length.

"There, that's how it works!" she announced, elbowing me for attention. "Look, Penny. It's thicker this way," Kyla explained. She turned to show her discovery to the block group. I was impressed that she worked tenaciously until she solved the problem. Choice Time provided her with the opportunity to persist.

Children often use Choice Time to further their learning in mature ways. Recently I worked with Cassie at Choice Time. A few days earlier during math, Cassie and I had had a discussion about her negligence in checking over mistakes in her independent math packet. She had many uncorrected problems. I asked Cassie if she would like to meet with me at Choice Time one day that week. I could sit beside her as she worked and help out if she needed any assistance. I told her that I had no Goals Conferences scheduled for Wednesday and Thursday, and that I would save one of those days for her if she liked. She considered the proposal for a moment and decided on Thursday. I was somewhat surprised. Cassie is not known for being conscientious about her work. I was glad that she chose to work on her math goal and that Choice Time would allow us a little extra time to work together. Thursday was three days away, however. I half expected that Cassie would promptly forget all about the plan. But when Thursday came, Cassie bounced in before school and signed up for Penny's Math. "See you later at Choice Time," she reminded me. We had a half hour together. We were the center of a little group who had signed up for Penny's Math. The Penny's Math option is for people in my math group who want to do independent problem-solving work in the math folders. Karen and Heidi sat beside us, and Robert was across the table. Mostly, I supported Cassie, who worked hard making corrections. Cassie made a mature decision that day, and she felt good about the results.

It takes time for the maturity that Cassie demonstrated to develop. When children are first confronted with making decisions and working independently, they don't always do it well. A second-year student, Jody, still has trouble deciding what she wants to do for Choice Time. Almost every morning she studies the choices, consults with her friends, poises the marker to write her name, changes her mind, goes to Jane's room to check on possibilities, and often uses up her before-school time without making a decision. She then must sacrifice some of Choice Time itself in deciding. I counsel her, "Jody, just pick something. If you don't like it, tomorrow is another day, and you can pick something different."

"I know," Jody replies. But still she hesitates. I don't know why, and I ponder ways to help her make decisions more easily. I trust that reminding her of the constancy of Choice Time will be a source of security that will eventually help.

Home/School Connections

The breadth of children's learning is wonderful to see. Our students constantly amaze us with what they know. They learn all the time and in all kinds of contexts: out and about with their families, at home, at friends' houses, on the bus, in the lunchroom, on the playground, and in our classrooms. We feel lucky to teach young children, who learn so spontaneously. *Teach* may be the wrong word, though. Often, we feel that our main responsibility is to help keep this learning going, rather than to interfere with it by trying to teach something.

We do try to capitalize on every learning opportunity the children present to us. And since many of their interests center on their homes and families, the links between home and school are excellent resources for learning. Supporting these links furnishes children with emotional scaffolding as well. Every day we see children making home/school connections during Choice Time.

Some of these connections are a direct result of things that occur at home that the children want to share or extend at school. The survival kit that Carter got for Christmas prompted him to sign up for Reading/ Writing/Drawing. He worked for two days using crayons to draw an elaborate picture of Grand Lake, his favorite place to go canoeing with his family. "I'm doing this because I want it to be summer," he confided to William, who sat next to him on the second day. He went on to explain why the water in his picture was two different colors of blue. "You can always tell the deep water because it is a darker color." Likewise, a family trip to Boston to see the Red Sox play resulted in Jonah creating a series of drawings to represent the event. His drawings of the game were very detailed, and he told me the stories that went with the pictures. I was impressed that the drawings had some recognizable objects and figures in them, as well as some interactions between them. They were very different from his usual drawings, which tended to be fairly nonrepresentational. One night Gordon looked at maps at home with his father. The next day at Choice Time he drew a map of his house. He began labeling the rooms with words ("Living Room," "Cichin"), and then he switched to initials. I asked him what rooms "WP" and "F" stood for, and he laughed. "Oh, those aren't rooms. That's down in the basement. *WP* for water pump, and *F* is for furnace!"

Often, children who have learned a new skill at home are anxious to teach it to their friends at school. Origami went up on the board as a choice after Ryan's family began learning how to do it at home. Ryan became adept at origami, and he instructed many of our students in the art of paper folding. Similarly, the day after our first snowstorm, Heidi became an instructor at Choice Time, teaching children how to cut paper to make snowflakes, as her mother had taught her the day before. Often the home learnings that children are most anxious to share are associated with our theme study of the moment. Cindy brought in her *How to Draw Dinosaurs* book when we studied dinosaurs and assisted children who wanted to learn to draw them. When we studied birds, Robert was the expert who coached other students in identifying the bird calls on the tape he brought to school. Choice Time is an excellent arena for children who want to share their expertise. We recognize that the children themselves are among our best resources as teachers.

Many of the children's parents join us at Choice Time to contribute their time and talents as well. Some of them come on a regular basis for one Choice Time period each week, allowing us to offer some choices that require adult supervision. Most years we have adult coverage of the workbench in Jane's room almost every day, so all the children have opportunities throughout the year to use woodworking tools to produce a real creation. Last year, Tricia's mom, Denise, came in once a week during the first half of the year to cook with a small group of children at Choice Time. We made great strides in taste-testing recipes for our pumpkin recipe book—until Denise got a new job that paid her real money! We cooked less regularly after that, but we still were able to continue our pumpkin recipe project and to produce all the treats for parties and special events with the help of various parents and grandparents to supervise the cooking area at Choice Time.

Workbench and cooking are traditional "home" occupations that our involved parents allow us to offer at school on a regular basis. We encourage parents and other relatives to come in at Choice Time to share their unique talents in other areas as well. For example, Krystal's mother came in twice a week for two months to organize and supervise the creation of a class quilt, in connection with our study of life long ago. A quilting bee was the culmination of this ambitious project. We welcome parents as "floaters" during Choice Time, too. Several parents come in weekly to help out and to be a part of whatever is going on at Choice Time that day.

For some children this time to be with a parent becomes very special. Henry's mother, Sarah, worried that Henry "hung on" her and monopolized her attention when she came to help out at Choice Time. He insisted that she sit with him and watch while he painted or drew, or that she alone play a game with him. "I'm not being much help to you," she apologized. I assured her that Henry's behavior was typical for a first-year student. He would let her become more involved with other children as time went on. Right now, how wonderful it was that Henry, the oldest of the three children in his family, could have his mother all to himself. And how wonderful for her to become a part of Henry's school life in this important way.

Young children think about their families a lot when they are at school. Happy as they are to be with their friends, many of our students acknowledge that they miss their families during the day. At Choice Time these children have an opportunity to work through their home-sickness. We see evidence of this in the letters that they write to family members, the pictures emblazoned with "I love you, Mom," and the special creations made at Constructions for parents or siblings. An unlimited number of children can sign up for Reading/Writing/Drawing, and there are often five or six children doing this choice in each room on any given day. We keep the paper shelves well stocked, and we always have stationery and envelopes of various sizes available. Envelopes seem to inspire letter writing! On a morning not long ago I watched Elizabeth write nine letters during Choice Time, one for each member of her two families, and one each for her dog and her cat. She sealed each letter up in its own envelope and carefully labeled and decorated them. I envied her. If only I could be such a good correspondent!

Our classrooms are very small. We wish that we had room for a permanent "housekeeping" corner. To substitute for a playhouse, Bryant's family has lent us a large furnished dollhouse, long and low, that rests on the floor under one bulletin board. This dollhouse, combined with a set of small blocks and farm figures, is a very popular choice for children of all ages. We have chests of dress-ups, too, for impromptu playacting. Our Little Room dramatic play area sometimes becomes a "house," when it is not being used as an authentic environment that we have simulated to go along with our theme under study. A third-year student, Curtis, was in there by himself at Choice Time the other day. I watched him for a moment through the Little Room window. He puttered happily with the pots and pans, a blue scarf from the dress-up chest tied around his neck. I knocked on the door and stuck my head in. "How's it going, Curt?"

"Good," he replied, smiling sweetly. "I'm just hanging out at home." We respect a child's need to "hang out" and to think about home from time to time during their school day. Choice Time gives us a chance to let it happen.

Socializing and Collaborating

One day Kyla and Jan were playing with the dollhouse at Choice Time. Casey and I were sitting together at a table nearby having a Goals Conference. Suddenly, Kyla was beside me, complaining bitterly that Jan wouldn't let her put down any of the rugs that belonged in the house. Jan was right behind her, "Those rugs are too thick. They look stupid with the furniture!" Kyla was willing to compromise and use a rug in only one of the rooms. Jan didn't think that was a good idea. That room was the kitchen, and rugs didn't belong in the kitchen. Maybe they could they have two kitchens, one without a rug and one with a rug, I suggested. No, there was not enough kitchen furniture for that! Realizing that my ideas were not going to be much help in solving this problem, I asked the girls to put the toys down and go to the kneeling table to talk about it. They needed to figure out a way they could both be happy and then come to tell me about it. If they needed any help, they could let me know. Jan and Kyla came back to me in a few minutes, the problem resolved. No rugs! Were they *both* happy with that decision? Yes, and indeed, both girls were all smiles. Though I wondered to myself if Kyla had gotten a raw deal, I restrained myself from trying to "make it better." They played happily (without rugs) the rest of Choice Time. I had trusted them to work it out on their own, and they did.

Whenever there are interactions between people, there are sure to be times of conflict mixed in with the smooth times. In our classrooms Choice Time is a sociable time; it is a time to practice becoming a functional society. When minor tiffs emerge, the children quickly become used to being asked to "go figure out a way you can both be happy." Jane and I are in the wings, on hand to help with a resolution if we are needed. But children rarely ask for our assistance, and we have learned over the years to intervene less and less in these small disagreements. It is not always easy to let go of our own logical ideas, not to insist that our adult recommendations are the best resolutions to children's problems. We have seen that the simple process of talking things over is magical. The less we interfere, the more consistently we see children resolving problems to their satisfaction without our help.

Not long ago I watched Carter, Bryant, and Ronnie, all second-year students, at Choice Time for a while. They were in the bench area playing with the big blocks and the jar of marbles. I first became aware of them when I heard Carter and Bryant discussing who should have a particular marble. Bryant wanted it, but Carter had gotten it first. Bryant was proposing the idea that sometimes people could take turns or give up what they wanted. Carter countered that he had the marble first, and he wasn't finished with it yet. They did not come to me to solve this problem for them—they simply spent some time discussing it, in very controlled terms. Obviously, they had heard civilized discussion and negotiation going on before. They were trying it out on their own. Since I was involved with a Goals Conference with another child, I didn't find out how they resolved the marble issue. I only know that there were no fireworks, and their play continued.

A little while later, I heard Carter and Bryant deeply involved in another discussion. It was actually a discussion—not an argument—centered upon their relationship with Ronnie (who was sitting and listening to the whole exchange). It seemed that there was some competition for Ronnie's affections. Carter complained to Bryant, "You always want Ronnie to be just with you." Later he said, "Why don't you invite *me* over sometime?" I did not hear all of their talk, but they spent quite a long time discussing. Eventually, they were playing again, each one creating his own block construction, but working together amiably.

I don't think that the two boys solved the issue of rivalry for Ronnie during this Choice Time. I'm not even sure they actually considered it to be a great big problem. At any rate, I was impressed to hear them discussing and airing some of their concerns. I'm sure that part of their willingness to do this kind of talking stemmed from their training at home. But another important factor that influenced the discussion was that the boys had *time* to have it. Time to talk is a scarce commodity in school. Perhaps the discussion could have occurred outside at recess, but not as easily. At recess, kids that age *run*, they expend energy. They don't slow down long enough to talk.

The Choice Time environment lends itself to discussions of this kind. It is a calm time. There is no set task or product to come out of Choice Time. There is little adult interference in the interactions of the kids. These boys were able to work through some feelings, right then, with no postponements. We feel that relaxed exchanges like these pay off in better relations between children in the future.

Usually, children get along very well in our classrooms. Because only a third of the children are "new" to the class each fall, there is a continuity of values and expectations, a family atmosphere that is unique in multiaged groups. Since the students in a multiage class are at different levels of development in all areas, the children expect to encounter diversity in their classmates. They learn to work together, to depend on each other for help, and to respect each others' differences. They learn that they each have an important voice and responsibility in creating a happy classroom community.

The spring weeks that we enjoyed *Charlotte's Web* for our theme spawned some wonderful collaborations. We had voted to turn the Little Room into Zuckerman's Barn. After conducting the initial brainstorming for ideas for how we could achieve this transformation, Jane and I gathered some supplies, and then we let the children sign up four at a time for "Make Zuckerman's Barn" as a choice. The next week various groups of children worked on the room during Choice Time. They made paper fences, barn doors, the hay loft, and the manure pile. They produced a box for Wilbur's trough, masks for all the animal characters, and Charlotte's web up in one corner. The children worked collaboratively to create the barn. The day came when it was finished. Serene, Cassie, Susan, and Kyla were the first to sign up for the Little Room. Their first job was to tidy up; then they could play in there. They were all busy, one with a broom and a dustpan, two of them stuffing scraps of paper into a plastic garbage bag. Serene made signs for the doors: ZUCKERMAN'S BARN. She checked her spelling from the *Charlotte's Web* book. She came to me wondering where the tape was, so that she could hang up the signs. She whispered loudly, "There's a snake in the barn trying to steal Charlotte!" The playing had already begun.

Another day three of the youngest kids, Carter, Rebecca, and Erin, added to the *Charlotte's Web* Bulletin Board at Choice Time. They made a big barn and various figures to go on the board. They were very self-sufficient as they made their cutouts, but they relied on Larry, who was playing with the bricks right below the bulletin board, to staple their things up. He commented to me at the end of Choice Time, "I was the only tall one around. I had to help them out."

Helping each other out is expected behavior in our classrooms. We allow five minutes at the end of Choice Time for cleaning up. We expect children to be responsible first for their own messes, but we encourage anyone who is not busy to pitch in and help someone else. Most children are willing helpers; they discover ways to make cleaning up fun. Gordon, Ronnie, and Mark put away the blocks assembly-line style. Hannah and Suzette pretend to be bunnies hiding food in their burrow as they stack the bricks on the shelves. For some of the children, cleaning up seems to be almost as much fun as Choice Time itself. Children who help others or work together to accomplish a task feel good about themselves. Choice Time provides many opportunities for children to build self-esteem.

Children in our classes count on each other for support. Most of them are sensitive to each other's needs. They are also protective of each other's rights. On one occasion Bryant signed up for Bricks two days in a row. Bryant is often one of the first children to get into the classroom, so he has first pick of the choices. Bricks are a very popular choice and limited to only two children at a time. We have no hard and fast rules to regulate signing up. Usually, it just works out. When Curtis came in and saw Bryant's name, he complained to Bryant, hoping to get him to erase his name. Instead, Bryant promised that he wouldn't sign up for Bricks the *next* day. Later, I heard others reminding Bryant that he should give someone else a turn tomorrow. "Okay, okay!" he assured them. All on their own they were regulating the Brick usage.

Another time, Thomas laughed at Erica, who was having trouble reading the choices as she was signing up. Jan jumped to Erica's defense, saying, "It wouldn't feel very good if you got laughed at if you couldn't read something." Later at Choice Time, Erica, Kyla, and Jan were play-ing blocks. Thomas was doing Constructions on the other side of the room. Kyla acted as emissary and came to report, "Erica is not your friend anymore. Erica is mad at you now."

Thomas responded, "Oh, I did one little thing and now she's mad!"

Kyla answered, "Maybe it wasn't such a little thing!" Case closed. Kyla left Thomas with something to think about.

Jane and I often see children working at bettering their classroom community. We have a subtle role in this process. The children are aware of our values and expectations; we frequently talk about them and we constantly model them. We try to influence children's behavior without being overly directive. When we see responsible behavior occur-ring, we are likely to make a casual comment about it. I watched Jenni-fer, Jan, and Karen getting ready to play a game at Choice Time recently. The game had been loaned to us by one of the children, and it was in rough shape. Before playing, the girls decided to repair the box and sort out the game pieces. I came over as they were taping the box lid's cor-ners and putting the game pieces in Baggies. I commented that I thought the extra attention they were giving to this poor old game would be appreciated by the class. "Yeah, now everything won't be falling out all over the place," Karen answered.

I watched as the girls rolled the die to see who would go first. "That's a good way to decide," I murmured as I moved on. I was impressed with the girls' display of initiative and caring. I let them know my feelings in an unobtrusive way. We find that it is not necessary to be heavy-handed in our compliments when children act appropriately. We know how *we* feel when we are praised effusively. "What's the big deal?" we think. After all, most of us know what we should do to be "good." The hard part is doing it, and that's the part we all keep working at.

Choice Time is designed to allow children to be with others or to be by themselves. Each day a surprising number of children, and it's not always the same ones, choose to work or play independently. Sometimes this time to be alone gives a child a chance to reflect on his or her own behavior. It was obvious that Andy was in a reflective mood one day at Choice Time. He signed up for Reading/Writing/Drawing, and he worked industriously to make a "Relaxing Cloud" for a friend outside of class. He said that he had one himself at home. On several pieces of paper stapled together he drew a cloud at the top with a computer under it. He taped on a long piece of yarn which hung down from the com-puter. "The cloud has a relaxing chair and a pool in it," he told me. He explained further. The idea was to tug on the string when you felt a need to calm down. The computer would tell you whether you should go ahead and keep doing what you were doing. Instead, maybe you needed to pretend to be sitting in the chair by the cool pool, just relaxing. "It works for me," Andy confided. "My mom thought it up."

Andy's method did seem to work for him, at least at Choice Time. Ordinarily, though, Choice Time is a peaceful time for most children. Kids go about their business in a relaxed way. In reading over my notes in my day book, I am struck by the number of times I begin my entry with this comment: "Choice Time was very mellow today." I wonder how important "mellowness" is for learning?

A Time to Learn

There is a perception among some educators and parents that a Choice Time is free time, and that it is not a time for significant learning. Recently, a kindergarten teacher came in to observe our program. She watched the whole-group Morning Message lesson with interest. However, as soon as the children broke up to go to their choices for Choice Time, she headed for the door, whispering, "I'll come back later when you're doing something." Her behavior indicated to us that she did not see a purpose in watching children engaged in independent activities.

For us, Choice Time has proven to be the setting for abundant growth and widespread learning among our students. However, we suspect that many of the visitors to our classrooms share this teacher's conviction that learning occurs only when children are being taught. We used to be nervous when visitors would walk into our rooms at Choice Time, thinking that they would assume that nothing important was going on. But mixed in with the physical, social, and emotional growth we see occurring in our students, we also see much evidence of academic growth. We're not uncomfortable when anyone drops in at Choice Time anymore. We know how much learning is happening.

My clipboard notes from a Choice Time one morning in March show the wide range of learning experiences the children typically create for themselves.

Choice Time Clipboard   March 14

Rebecca, Carter, and Jacob— All were playing with big blocks. Each child had his or her own thing going though. Carter was making a palace (with two entrances—one secret). Jacob had built a long ramp (maybe two feet), down which he slid a marble, which hit a small block and knocked over a little man on the other side. He was eager to show me how it worked. Rebecca worked on a dungeon—she had enclosed a little Lego man in her block structure, complete with roof.

Erin—Sat at a little table next to the Big Block group (probably so she could be close to Rebecca), working on her Family Book. It's beautifully illustrated with Cray-Pas. She's done a page for what she likes to do with each member of her family.

Ronnie and Cassie— Were using the Sta-blox, but Ronnie was usually under the table visiting with Susan and Bryant who were playing with bricks.

Susan and Bryant—Made big towers with bricks. Susan wanted to measure hers and got the measuring tape on her own. I helped her to start at zero.

Thomas—Sitting by himself with paper and scissors, folding and cutting. He brought in a book today about making paper airplanes. He had designed his own plane and had made up a set of instructions and written them out for Grady, who is now in the intermediate multiage.

Serene and Kenneth—Were in the puppet theater, using the stick puppets we had made of *Charlotte's Web* characters. "We're making up funny puppet shows, doing everything backwards."

Curtis and Elizabeth—Goal-review conferences with me. Curtis reviewed goals with me. Elizabeth was supposed to, but we didn't get that far. She illustrated her newly published book instead. She was getting some help reading her story from a visiting prospective parent. She illustrated carefully with colored pencils.

Scott—Doing spider research. Making a book.

Erica and Jan—Reading/Writing/Drawing. It took them quite a while to get settled down. They were going to write cards, and Erica delivered one to me. "Dear Penn I Love you you Are a good teacher." She came to me with her dictionary for "Teacher."

Frances—Finishing the book she started at Investigations the other day, "A Charlotte's Cousin Adventure." She was asking for help with words from Erica and Jan.

Gordon—Was signed up to work on Bricks with Bryant, but Richard (a sixth-grade helper) came down and Gordon opted to edit his snowmobiling story with him. It's the first story he has published, and he has been excited about his writing lately. He was anxious to edit.

Samuel and Larry—Playing checkers.

Maryann, Warren, and Daniel—Cooked pumpkin pudding with Denise. She did a good job involving the kids today, letting them do the work, helping them with the thinking. She praised them often—they were doing such good measuring and thinking. How much would a can of pumpkin (15 ounces) measure up to be? Maryann, Warren, and Daniel were all very involved—there was no straying from the cooking area. "The dishes are over there ready for you to wash," Denise told them, and they got right into it. We've had to work with Denise a bit, helping her with involving the kids, letting them do the work, and making the recipe reading and measuring a learning situation.

On this one day a wealth of problem solving and literacy learning was occurring. Children were also involved in dramatic play, in discovering spatial relationships, and in communicating orally. Some of them were making artistic creations. There was no doubt that learning was going on.

The tricky thing for some educators and parents to accept is the randomness of the learning that occurs at Choice Time. It is difficult to pin it down and make it fit into a curriculum guide or a scope and sequence chart. These adults wonder: Can all the students be getting what they need? Kids have free time at home. Shouldn't teachers be using precious school time to teach them the things they need to know?

Admittedly, there are many times during the day when we guide our students: "Okay, now you will listen. Now you will discuss. Now you will read. Now you will write. Now you will problem solve. Now you will think mathematically." Though we try to allow children to have as much control of their learning as possible within these frameworks, we are still in charge of the agenda. We continually look for ways to shift more and more ownership to the children.

Jane and I are convinced that children can be trusted to choose learning opportunities on their own. Having seen how much they learn at Choice Time makes us even more committed to the possibilities of student choice. Choice Time gives students a chance to be in charge, to develop their intellects, to pursue personal interests. Once in a while we share a bittersweet laugh together when we remember the visiting teacher who promised to come back when we were "doing something." We liken her to the principal who schedules an appointment to observe our class for evaluation purposes. She wants to be sure to come at a time when she can see the teacher teaching a lesson. It seems to Jane and me that educators and parents should be looking in classrooms for evidence that kids are learning, rather than that teachers are teaching. Setting up the environment so that kids learn is the most important thing that teachers can do, but so often that is not what is recognized as the goal of teaching. We work hard to reverse the misconception that children must be taught in order to learn.

Our students often help us to envision possibilities for learning. In the spring of his first year in our class, Bryant sat with Thomas at Choice Time one day. He had signed up for Reading/Writing/Drawing, and he had a piece of paper in front of him. He wasn't using it much; he was watching Thomas work on an "adventure" book. He said to me as I came close, "Penny, I just thought up a new choice—Chatting. You can sign up for it and then go around the room chatting to people. You can find out what everybody's doing." I told Bryant that I liked the idea.

I put *Chatting* up for a choice the next day. Bryant signed up. He explained the choice to the other kids at our Morning Meeting. "I call it Chatting. Chatting means that you talk to someone for a while. You walk around talking to people. You could talk about *Charlotte's Web* or anything."

"Why is chatting important?" I asked Bryant.

He thought for a moment. "Because sometimes talking helps you to get more air," Bryant responded.

Jane asked, "What should someone do if he or she is busy and someone comes by to chat?"

Rosa answered that question. "You would say, 'Could you please go over and chat with someone else and come back when I'm done?'"

So it was a plan. Bryant chatted with several people at Choice Time that first day. He came and stood next to Serene and me when we were having a Goal Conference. He listened to Serene read for a minute or two, then he moved on. Andy fussed at him for staying and chatting with his group at Big Blocks for so long. "We're trying to concentrate here!" But I observed other children welcoming Bryant and conversing briefly when he came by.

Serene noticed me watching Bryant. "I'm going to sign up for Chatting tomorrow," she said.

I thought about Chatting later. What a civilized concept! And what a novel notion to legitimize talking in the classroom. The idea of designating time to chat, to observe and interact with the community, is typically unheard of in school. Usually, chatting is relegated to the playground. I thought, too, about Bryant's rationale for chatting as a choice: "talking helps you to get more air." I wondered how often children feel stifled in school. What else can we do to give them more room to breathe?

Making Choices in School   3

Penelle Chase

"When we finish our study of mammals in a few weeks, you can each decide on an activity to do to share something you have learned. Soon we'll brainstorm a big list of choices. Let's all be thinking of possibilities!"

"You need to make a choice, Gary. We are being distracted by you. Do you want to stay here with the group or go to a planning chair to figure out a way you can act that won't bother the people around you?"

"There has been lots of good writing going on in this classroom lately. People have been choosing interesting topics. Today we'll talk about how people are coming up with their ideas."

"Children, we can do something special for our end-of-the-year celebration. Here are some thoughts we had. We could go to the children's museum in Augusta, or . . . go for a hike up Mount Battie, or . . . try out the new miniature golf course in town. Any other ideas? It's your choice!"

Choice is a big word. It has a multitude of meanings. As Jane and I focus on opportunities for choice in our classrooms, we become very conscious of what we are calling "choice." There are many different kinds of choosings going on. Sometimes we *give* children choices; sometimes we allow children to *make* choices for themselves. Though we see value in providing options of all kinds, we weigh our choice offerings. We realize that choice is a continuum that extends from specifying a narrow range of possibilities to allowing children free rein to choose options for themselves. Sometimes we are happy with the choices we offer; sometimes we are embarrassed that we have referred to certain options as choices! Giving kids choices and letting them make decisions is not always easy. Often we applaud the decisions the children make; other times we wish they had chosen differently. We are still considering and questioning how much choice in school is just the right amount. On a daily basis we think about the choices we offer and the choices the children make.

Penny's Day Book   January 28

A few notes about various kids and their choices lately.

1/24—Carter and Henry have chosen to sit with each other often during Communications Workshop recently. On this day our student teacher, Brooke, noticed that they were doing some talking at Quiet Writing Time and had asked them, "Does one of you need to sit somewhere else?" Carter responded, "No, we're doing okay." Brooke observed that the boys did do "okay" for the remainder of Quiet Writing Time, but that they were very animatedly discussing and not writing for most of the rest of Communications Workshop. Carter said to Henry at sharing time, "I don't think we can sit next to each other tomorrow. I usually get lots of pages done, but today I didn't." They decided to sit apart tomorrow.

1/27—Rebecca's cubby was overflowing. I suggested that she might want to sign up to clean out her cubby at Choice Time tomorrow. Okay, she agreed, she would sign up now for cleaning her cubby, so she wouldn't forget it tomorrow morning. The next morning at Choice Time I noticed that Rebecca immediately began working on a big card. "To Pop-pop," she painted on the front of it. She showed me the inside, done with marker: "Roses are red, vilets are blue, I love you." Fifteen minutes into Choice Time she left her work and went to clean her cubby. She said to me: "I was signed up for two things, Reading, Writing, and Drawing and Clean Cubby. I knew that, but I wanted to make this card for my Pop-pop, because he is in the hospital. I'll glue this cover on after it dries." She went off to clean her cubby (which took five minutes at most—I didn't inspect it!), then she went happily back to work on her card. She proudly showed me the finished product. I have no doubt that Rebecca had not forgotten that she had signed up to clean her cubby when she signed up for Reading, Writing, Drawing— she figured she'd get to the cleaning chore if she had time. She had made a choice for herself—making the card for her grandfather was more important than cleaning her cubby. I can't help but agree.

Last week Jennifer worked on a card for her swimming instructor, who had been in an automobile accident and was badly hurt. She worked on it for two days at Communications after she finished writing in her day book. She didn't share it with me or even tell me that she was doing it. Her mom asked me if I had seen the card when she picked Jennifer up one afternoon. Jennifer had her big card with her in her backpack ready to take home. Jennifer had done her communicating for real reasons; it was something she needed to do and nobody else had anything to do with it. I am glad that she had the time to do a meaningful job like this in school.

On Thursday I was taking down the children's writing topics. When I asked Bryant what he would write about, he replied without hesitation, "Jammin' it." I asked no further questions; Bryant often wrote stories about his prowess on the basketball court. He produced this story: "I hv Ban haning to Gt ther. thn it hpnD. it ws 1 spl mv. I Das DclLe LfiD My FEt AF thE GrnD AND I FLo Fro the Ar For the duNK." (I have been training to get there. Then it happened. It was one simple move. I just delicately lifted my feet off the ground, and I flew through the air for the dunk.) It is an impressive story because of the suspense, the great words. I think Bryant is internalizing some of our mini-lesson work lately. Jane had written a story about going to Boston—we used it to discuss adding details and using interesting words. We also recently put up a lead that Erin had written and discussed her word usage, her lovely figures of speech. Bryant described his one incredible move in basketball, expanding his idea beautifully. He will be featured to help with the mini-lesson on Monday. It is great to see some of the things we bring out in mini-lessons being translated into the children's own writing.

It was Brooke's last day Friday. After we had done Popsicles, and cards from the children, and presents, Jane asked if anyone wanted to say something special to Brooke. Several children thanked her for this and that, and others said that they would miss her. Then Roger was called on. "I have just a little poem. 'Roses are red, violets are blue, and I will miss you.' I got that idea from Rebecca."

Sometimes we wonder how we got so hooked on the concept of student choice. We suspect that working with a multiaged group has been a factor. While a broad range of developmental levels is the norm in a graded classroom, the breadth of this range is even more pronounced in a multiage grouping. It has required us to offer many choices in order to meet the needs of all the children. But choosing where to sit, when to clean, what to write, and how to show someone you care are important choices in any context. We know that the two main goals we have for our students are that they be happy and that they learn. We believe that happiness and learning are connected. We think that children who have ownership of their learning are happier and are more likely to learn.

Sometimes visitors to our programs tell us, "Your classrooms are just so different from what we expected. With all those ages together and all the choices the children have, you'd think it would be confusing and chaotic, but it isn't. It's really very structured! Everyone knows what to do. And the children are so calm and good to each other! How do you do it?"

We think student ownership is the key to an orderly, caring classroom. The differences between our classrooms and other student-centered classrooms are subtle. Gradually over the years we have allowed the students to assume more and more control over their behavior and their education. They are responsible, in a large part, for the underlying "structure" that exists in our program. They have become skilled at managing themselves.

Over time we have seen our students become increasingly self-directed as we, the teachers, have adjusted our own roles in the classroom. Instead of determining the learning program by dispensing information, we now work at creating optimum conditions for learning. Instead of attempting to control student behavior, we now work with children to establish a caring community. In making these changes, we continually think of our own schooling and what works best for us as learners. We also consider the strengths and various learning styles of the children. We strive to make education in our classrooms feel natural and right for everyone. So far, the setting that we have found most effective is an open workshop that offers the children many alternatives. By allowing them to work at their own pace and to set their own goals, we are shifting the responsibility for learning and behavior to the children.

We are in process. Each year we make new discoveries about student ownership and empowerment. In this chapter I take a comprehensive look at our students as they move through a day at school. I describe some of their choices and the ways in which they are routinely encouraged to direct themselves on a daily basis. Over the course of their day at school, our students make many decisions. Some of these decisions are small ones; others are more substantial. The sum total of the decisions that the children make as a matter of course every day become a powerful element in their education.

A Day in School

Our daily schedule is slightly different each year. We share our school with forty-six other classrooms, so we do not have complete control over when we will do what. We aim for large blocks of uninterrupted time, as does every other teacher in our school. Often we have to take several deep breaths and recognize that we must "live with" inconvenient timing for our special physical education, music, art, computer, and library classes. Fortunately, Jane and I can usually arrange for all of our students to be occupied outside the classroom during the same time period, allowing us time to plan together. Other than that, all we can do is try to streamline our schedule, so that transition time is minimal. This is the schedule we follow this year.

Monday Through Thursday Mornings

8:05–8:20	Social Time
8:20–8:40	Talking Journal

8:40–9:10	Morning Meeting (sharing, poems, songs, Morning Message, announcements)
9:10–9:45	Choice Time
9:45–10:30	Investigations Workshop
10:30–10:50	Recess
10:50	Dismissal for five-year-olds
10:50–11:30	Math Groups (Children work in developmental groups)
11:30–11:35	Prepare for Communications Workshop
11:35–11:55	Lunch

Monday Through Thursday Afternoons

12:00–1:00	Communications Workshop—Reading Segment (story, quiet reading, reading with a friend, mini-lesson)
1:00–1:45	Mon.—Math Workshop; Computer Lab for 3rd- and 4th-year students (every other week) Tues.—Phys. Ed. (Jane's Class); Music (Penny's Class) Wed.—Art (Jane's Class); Phys. Ed. (Penny's Class) Thurs.—Writing Segment of Communications Workshop
1:45–2:30	Communications Workshop—Writing Segment (quiet writing in day books, collaborative writing, handwriting, research, sharing) Thursdays— Handwriting
2:30–2:40	End of the Day Circle
2:45	Dismissal

Friday Mornings

8:05–8:20	Social Time
8:20–8:40	Talking Journal
8:40–9:10	Choice Time
9:15–9:45	Library/Two Literature Groups
9:45–10:15	Library/Two Literature Groups
10:15–10:30	Songs, Poems, etc.
10:30–10:50	Recess
10:50	Dismissal for five-year-olds
10:50–11:30	Math Groups
11:30–11:35	Prepare for Communications Workshop
11:35–11:55	Lunch

Friday Afternoons

12:00–1:00	Communications Workshop—Reading Segment (story, quiet reading, reading with a friend, mini-lesson)
1:00–1:45	Communications Workshop—Writing Segment (quiet writing in day books, collaborative writing, handwriting, research, sharing)
1:50–2:35	Music (Jane's Class); Art (Penny's Class)
2:35–2:40	End of the Day Circle
2:45	Dismissal

During a normal day, our students make many decisions that impact their learning and govern their behavior. Here's how a typical day goes.

Before School

Our students choose whether they want to come into the classroom before school or go out onto the playground. Since our school has almost nine hundred students and the playground is crowded in the morning, most of our children opt to come straight to the classroom. Kids dribble in sporadically as the buses arrive. After they have hung up their outdoor clothing, they go first to their homeroom to take their name clips off the attendance chart. Then they decide how to occupy themselves. Mostly, they socialize and "hang out" in either of our connected rooms. They talk to each other, share some news with Jane or me, or go back and forth through the Little Room that joins our classrooms to see who's arrived at school. Often Jane and I have small jobs that need doing, and we have come to depend on the children's help. We can usually find someone who is eager to staple, deliver notes, return library books, or do the myriad other tasks that we used to do ourselves. Sometimes children draw or read, catch up on unfinished projects, or tidy cubbies. Often they show each other things they have brought from home. The children are free to do quiet activities of their choice.

At this before-school time we encourage the children to sign up for a choice to do later at Choice Time. They consider the choices listed on the Choice boards in both rooms. Some of them have already decided what they will choose and sign up quickly; others wait for friends to come in so they can discuss their plans. It is a relaxed time of day. The peace is interrupted when the bell rings, and the rest of our students and the children from the six other classes in our pod come into the common area en masse.

Talking Journal

As the arrival hubbub dies down, the newcomers sign up for Choice Time. The students who are in charge of filling out the attendance slip check the attendance chart to see if any clothespin name clips still remain. If so, they write the names of these absentees on the slip and hang it outside our doors, ready to be picked up and taken to the office. All the children return to their homerooms to get ready for Talking Journal. In my room we meet on low benches which are arranged in a circle. In Jane's room the children sit on the rug in a circle. Most of our gathering times occur in these two areas. The children choose who they will sit beside for Talking Journal circle. We recognize that choosing companions ensures security. Each morning a different child is the moderator at Talking Journal Time. The moderator chooses the speakers for Talking Journal. We raise our hands to be called on to share news or to show something we have brought from home. The moderator may make comments or ask questions of the sharer, and she also calls on other listeners to give their input. Jane and I used to moderate the Talking Journal sessions, until we realized that the children could easily assume this leadership role. At the conclusion of Talking Journal, the leader chooses the moderator for the next day. It is time for our Morning Meeting, and we form a loose line to go through the Little Room to join Jane and her students.

Morning Meeting

We all gather assembly-style, facing the message chart in the big open space in Jane's room. Again, children choose where they will sit. However, Jane and I qualify this choice as we remind the children as they get settled, "Sit where you will be a good listener and learner." One of us will lead the meeting that day and the other will observe, noting positive behaviors and contributions of the children. We consult our list to see whose turn it is to be the student observer for the meeting. The student observer also watches the group and records her impressions on Post-its. Our meeting begins with announcements by the children or the teachers. Then we spend a few minutes enjoying songs, poems, and chants before the message. These readings usually are connected to the theme we are currently studying; we welcome the children's input in finding appropriate pieces. Often, the children have discovered the selections in their reading, and we have copied them on charts to present to the children. It's even better when a child writes an original piece, copies it on chart paper, and illustrates it herself. She will be in charge of presenting the piece to the class at Meeting time.

Next, we turn to the message. The message is a letter to the children, which Jane and I have composed and transcribed onto chart paper. Five or six words are left partially blank with only the beginning sound given. We read the message aloud with the children, deciding together which words will make sense in the blanks. The message is a real-life communication that serves as a vehicle for initiating topics for discussion. The message is often connected to our theme; it sometimes suggests the focus of the day's activities. As we discuss the content of the message, we note word meanings and usage, conventions of grammar, and other stylistic features of the writing. Next, students volunteer to spell the missing words. As we spell we discuss the sound/symbol correspondence of standard spelling. We compare "sound spellings" to the conventional spellings of words.

As we review the message we invite children to point out interesting things they have noticed. The students' "noticings" help to direct the lesson and lead to discussions on a wide variety of literacy concepts: word patterns, rhymes, homophones, vowel combinations, blends, mechanical features of punctuation and capitalization, etc. We find that many times the things the students bring up are things we would have "taught" ourselves. We usually have time to concentrate on certain things we want them to notice as well. The learnings that come out of a message are not preplanned; each message lends itself to different noticings by the children.

At the end of the message discussion both the teacher and the student observer read from their Post-its, commenting on the discoveries or behaviors of several of the children. Remarks from adults ("Erica realized that she would have a hard time listening sitting next to Rosa, so she got up and moved to another spot," and "Ronnie heard all the consonants when he sound-spelled *interesting* for the message") and from students ("I heard Curtis's voice really loud when we were reading the message together," and "Tanya found two words that rhyme on the message— *show* and *know*") reaffirm the expectations we have for message time. Each day one of children files these Post-its in the appropriate students' sections in the class record books.

A copy of the message is sent home daily for homework and to provide information about school activities to parents. We expect parents to interact with their children while doing the homework, and we encourage the children to "notice" things for their parents as they do in class. Often the homework poses a question or an idea that children may choose to respond to by writing and/or drawing on the back of the paper. Together parents and students can explore and extend things we are learning about in school. Our Morning Meeting ends, I head back to Room 106, and the children disperse to whichever room they have chosen for Choice Time.

Choice Time

The children have signed up for their choice of activities before Talking Journal Time. There are a wide variety of choices; some of them are teacher ideas and others have been suggested by the children. Some of the choices are regular offerings and others change as our themes change. Examples of choices include: blocks, puzzles, games, reading, writing, drawing, painting, constructions, clay, math tubs, dramatic play in the Little Room, etc.

The Choice Time period is structured so that children can work and play either independently or in groups. Once every two or three weeks each student is scheduled to meet with the teacher for a goal-setting conference during Choice Time. This conference is the only intrusion upon the children's choice of activities.

The children are independent at Choice Time. They know how to set up their activities, where to get materials, and how to clean up after themselves. Snack time is part of Choice Time, too, so children visit the snack table, consult the board to see "how many," and choose from the two or three offerings of the day. Parents supply us with boxes of graham crackers, pretzels, and other healthy snacks.

Jane and I are involved with Goal Conferences with two students each, and the other children are responsible for themselves at Choice Time. They know the routine, they know the expectations, and they know to help each other. Of course, there are occasional interruptions from children who need to tell or show us something "right now," but these interruptions are not distracting. Choice Time is easygoing. It has become a valued and important part of our day.

Investigations Workshop

We have Investigations Workshops four times a week. During this forty-five-minute period we work on theme-related activities. The themes we study are based on a three-year cycle of our school district's science and social studies curriculum for the kindergarten, first, and second grades. The workshop choices include large-group, small-group, and individual projects. Sometimes Jane and I determine the groupings; other times the students choose the activity or group in which they wish to participate. Hands-on activities that require the students to solve problems, experiment, and do research are major components of the Investigations Workshop. Whenever possible, Jane and I participate in the workshop activities alongside the children. We all have investigations logs to record reflections and significant learnings.

Depending on the theme under study, Investigations activities vary a great deal. One very successful theme, the Art Gallery, occupied us for six or seven weeks. Our activities included visiting a gallery, touring an art museum, talking to artists, reading books about art and artists, experimenting with light and color, looking at many reproductions of great artwork, and making art ourselves. Though there are no "typical" opportunities for choice in any one theme study, here are some examples of ways students assumed ownership of their learning in the Art Gallery theme.

- We exposed the children to the works of many different artists, periods, and genres. We gave the children opportunities to experiment with a variety of media to make art: colored pencils, cut paper, clay, watercolors, pastels, charcoal. They kept all of their work in large oak tag portfolios.

- We read a book about color aloud. Then the students made crayon pictures to express emotions using color.

- Kids looked at the many reproductions displayed around the classrooms and worked in pairs discussing how the artists used color to communicate in the works. They wrote their ideas in their investigations logs.

- We read books about how artists use shape and line in their work. The children then experimented with shapes and lines in their own drawings.

- We decided that we would transform the Little Room into an artists' studio for this theme. First we brainstormed possibilities, and then we voted. It was a close vote between a sign shop and an artists' studio. For several days children signed up at Choice Time to help outfit the Little Room with the supplies needed in a studio. When the room was ready, *Artists' Studio* was added to the choices on the choice board. Four artists at a time could work independently in the studio at Choice Time.

- We looked at many examples of reproductions of still lifes and discussed them. Then the children each found objects around the room, arranged them, and made pencil sketches of their still lifes.

- We read *St. George and the Dragon* to the children and studied the reproduction of a painting by the same name. Kids then had a choice of activities to respond to the painting: making clay groupings of the important figures in the work; writing about what might have happened next in the picture; studying the various trees in the painting and using pastels to draw trees;

studying the figures in the painting and using colored pencils to draw a detail of a head.

- We discussed the Renaissance period and listened to recordings of Renaissance music. Children chose between movement and sound activities as a follow-up.

- We listened to Mussorgsky's *Pictures at an Exhibition* and learned about the work by reading the album cover. We drew pictures of our impressions of the music as we listened to the work again.

- The students each chose two pieces of art from their portfolios to exhibit for our Opening. They used construction paper to create frames for these pieces, and they thought of titles for their choices. They made cards to affix to their works, indicating the artist's name and the title of the piece. The titles sounded very professional!

- Several children did independent research on artists of their choice.

- We each made facsimiles of blue and red ribbons out of paper and "judged" the reproductions displayed in the classrooms. We defended our first and second choices in small-group discussions.

- We offered several books about artists as choices for Literature Group books.

- We discussed and voted on the refreshments we would have for our Opening and completed a shopping list. The children created invitations for their parents. We decided what music we would play at our Opening. Children chose how they would help to get ready for the Opening. Some children helped me hang the artworks in the library. Others helped Jane fix the snacks, cutting cheese, arranging fruit, putting crackers in baskets, and decorating the tables.

- As a wrap-up we asked the children to write and draw in their investigations logs. To get them thinking, we asked these questions: What did you learn? What was your favorite part of the theme? What was easy? What was hard?

Choices of activities, choices of companions, and choices about how to demonstrate what you know are usually features of Investigations Workshop. However, our theme work is infused into much of what we do all day long; it is by no means limited to Investigations time. Our students have a great deal of input into the direction of our work.

Literature Groups

On the one day of the week that we do not have Investigations Workshop, we have Literature Groups. Literature Groups are composed of ten students and one adult, a teacher or parent, who meet together to enjoy and discuss a book of their choice. Jane and I select examples of quality literature, as many titles as there are groups. On sign-up day we give short book talks to introduce the students to the upcoming Literature Group selections. The children sign up for their first and second preferences, and we make up the literature groups according to the students' choices. The Literature Groups meet for an hour-long session each week. Groups meet for five weeks. We study a variety of genres throughout the year, and the makeup of the groups changes with each new series of books.

During the sessions the children work on listening and speaking goals, as well as on a variety of literacy activities. Often the students help to determine the direction of the group. Some possible Literature Group activities are: comparing different versions of the story; listening to related books; reading with a partner; studying character, plot, setting, and style; examining vocabulary; and doing research. We all have literature logs to record our responses to books we read.

During the fourth Literature Group session each literature group works together to plan and create a culminating project to share with the other groups. On presentation day we enjoy a variety of creative responses to the good books we have read. Plays, puppet shows, demonstrations, murals, readings, posters, displays, and cooking ventures are common choices for Literature Group projects.

Math

The students are divided into two developmental groups for math class. We do large-group lessons, small-group lessons, and individual work in these sessions. The developmental groupings allow us to explore basic math concepts with children at similar stages. As much as possible we devise problems that are related to real-life situations. For example, in the spring we ask one of the groups to decide how much pumpkin seed of each variety we need for planting our annual pumpkin crop. We work together to calculate prices and order the seed. Then, the students compute the garden space needed and design a layout for the pumpkin patch. Another time one math group took on the responsibility of arranging for snacks for a whole-pod function. We calculated the number of children to be served, the amount of food needed, and the total cost. Whenever opportunities to make mathematical connections to our daily lives present themselves, we capitalize on them in math class.

We also work with students to create problems related to our current theme study. Designing good problems is as important as being able to solve them. When we read *Farmer Boy* by Laura Ingalls Wilder during our study of life long ago, we envisioned mathematical problems that Almanzo may have experienced. Both teachers and children wrote math challenges, and we solved each other's problems. We search for mathematical links in all of our theme work. When we study dinosaurs or space or weather, we base math problems on the scientific data we discover.

On Mondays we spend an hour of our Communications time in Math Workshop. Math Workshop also gives the students opportunities to work individually or in multiaged collaborative groups. Students choose freely from eight to twelve problem-solving activities offered at each workshop. For example, on a day in March we offered the following Math Workshop choices:

Survey: Decide on a survey question, collect data from the class, and make a display of the results.

M&M Math: Follow the directions in the M&M math book.

Cuisenaire Rods: Use the rods to answer the questions on the worksheet.

Pattern Block Shapes: Fill in the shapes on the pattern block puzzle papers and color them appropriately.

Battleship Game: Use the grid to locate your opponent's ships.

Math Mystery: Make a drawing that satisfies all the requirements of the Spring Scene problem.

Measuring: Measure this collection of objects and other things of your choice using both centimeters and inches. Record your results.

Fill the Cube Game: Fill a Unifix cube with corn and predict the number of kernels you used. Divide the kernels into groups of ten as you count and record your results. Repeat using lentils. Try predicting and counting corn and lentils as you fill other small containers.

Using Balance Scales: Find out how many of the following objects weigh as much as ten Unifix cubes: links, red pattern blocks, yellow pattern blocks, tan pattern blocks, beads, tiles. Record your results.

Shape Pictures: Use the cut outs of geometric shapes to make a picture or design. Glue your picture onto a piece of construction paper.

The last ten or fifteen minutes of Math Workshop are spent writing and drawing in investigations logs. We ask the children to reflect on what they discovered during that day's workshop and to describe their thought processes as they made their discoveries. Students volunteer to share their logs, and we discuss each other's reflections at the close of the workshop.

The concepts we address in both the developmental math groups and the Math Workshop are based on our school district's math curriculum requirements. We use manipulatives to demonstrate concepts, and we encourage children to use concrete materials regularly to help them understand mathematical abstractions.

Getting Ready for Communications Workshop

Math period ends and it is lunch time. A flurry of activity ensues as children get ready for our Communications Workshop, which follows lunch. The children return to their homerooms to visit their cubbies, where their writing folders are stored. The writing folder is a pocket folder which contains a day book, a personal dictionary, and a sheet listing the student's Communications Workshop Goals. Sometimes students store books they are currently reading in these folders, too.

After students get their writing folders from their cubbies, they go to the room that they have selected for Communications Workshop. The students have chosen whether they will have workshop in Jane's room or in my room and have signed up to be in that room for a two-week time period. The format for the workshop is the same in both rooms; the biweekly sign-up is based on the students' individual preferences. Some students alternate between rooms, some stay in one room consistently, and others base their decisions on their friends' plans.

The children are buzzing as they decide where they will sit for Communications Workshop and deposit their folders and pencils at the tables of various sizes and shapes around the room. Their places "saved," they go off to pick out the books they will read during workshop. There are many choices of reading materials. Some of the children head for the bookshelves, where books are identified with colored tape on the spines to represent the groupings: science, reference, social studies, poetry, fiction. Others peruse the books related to our theme, which are marked and displayed separately. Some children sort through baskets of collections of books: "little books," "new books," "Penny's Favorites," series by the Wright Group and Rigby Press, and magazines. The children choose up to six books to start with, and they place their stacks with their writing materials. Jane and I are busy now, too. We are gathering our own Communications Workshop materials. I get my day book from my cubby and search in my school bag for the novel that I brought from home. In all this commotion we are reminding children, "If you are working on certain books for your goals, don't forget to have those books at your place." "Make sure your pencil is sharpened." "Only six books, Trish.

There's not enough room on the table for that huge pile. You can get more when you finish your first six!" The dust settles as children gather to go to the cafeteria. When we return from lunch, we will be able to ease calmly into Communications Workshop.

Communications Workshop

Communications Workshop occurs every afternoon. It is a large block of time in which we are all engaged in a variety of literacy activities. We focus on the fundamentals of literacy: reading, writing, listening, speaking. Students and teachers make choices within these areas during Communications Workshop. Students work on the personal literacy goals that we have helped them develop during the goal-setting conferences at Choice Time. The structure of the workshop is standard. There is a reading segment and a writing segment each day. During both of these segments there is a quiet time when we all work independently and an interactive time when we converse and collaborate. Through trial and error over the years we have arrived at this combination of silence and sociability. All of us have opportunities during the workshop to study in an atmosphere that suits our individual learning styles.

Directly after lunch we begin the workshop with a read-aloud from a picture book, magazine, nonfiction book, or a continuing chapter book. We often read theme-related books at this time. The students help to choose from the selection we have gathered from the public and school libraries, from our classroom shelves, and from the children's home libraries. Sometimes we get together in Jane's room and listen in a large group. Other times Jane and I each read aloud in our respective rooms.

After the story we take a few minutes for status of the class. At this time we each share our writing topic for the day, along with a writing goal we plan to work on. Then we are all set for Quiet Writing Time later in the workshop. We note on our clipboards the children's writing topics for the day. The children have free choice of topics. The only requirement is to "Write about something important to you." Round-robin sharing of topics focuses the children and starts the rehearsal process for many of them. It saves time later when we begin to write. We suspect that students do some subconscious preplanning about their writing as they are involved with their reading. One day our story was very long and the children became itchy, so I sent them off without doing status of the class. Adam came to me at the beginning of writing time, wondering why we had skipped it. I explained my reasoning. "Now I don't know *what* I'm writing about," he murmured as he went off to think. A few other children came to me with the same problem. We've learned; we try not to bypass this good opportunity for children to organize their thoughts.

The reading segment of the workshop comes first. Reminding the students to "look over your goals sheets before you start your reading," we send them off to their chosen places. We begin with a Quiet Reading time in which we read and look at books independently. We insist that this time be silent. We want to provide an opportunity for readers to get "lost" in their books, without the well-intentioned interference from others who want to share what they are reading. After Quiet Reading Time, the reading segment of Communications Workshop continues with a variety of activities in every corner of the room. Some students enjoy partner reading. Now, friends may pair up to share books they have enjoyed. Sharing includes showing pictures, inventing a story to go with the pictures, talking about the book, or reading the book aloud. Another popular activity is to read and sing favorite poems and songs from the students' poetry notebooks. These notebooks are three-ring binders that contain copies of most of our Morning Meeting readings. Some students listen to cassette tapes of books at the Listening Center at this time. Others continue to read independently or to conduct research on self-chosen topics.

A ten-minute mini-lesson follows the reading time. The mini-lessons focus on reading and writing skills and strategies and on procedural elements of the workshop. Usually, we come together as a whole group for this lesson, and Jane and I do the lesson together. The two of us like to model, demonstrate, and role-play in our discussions of literacy. We believe that it is good for the children to see and hear our interactions. In one lesson Jane and I had a short discussion about passages we had noted in our reading that day that struck us as being powerfully written. "Look," Jane said, "I wrote down the page number on my bookmark here, so I could read it to you. Listen." After Jane read, we discussed how that writing had "spoken" to her and what elements of it she could apply to her own writing. We continued our modeling by discussing the passage I had chosen. We then suggested that the next day the students might note on bookmarks examples of excellent writing they found in their reading. We planned to spend some mini-lesson time sharing their discoveries.

Students help to orchestrate many of the mini-lessons. Often we use children's published or in-process work to illustrate features of good writing. Sometimes, children verbalize their successful reading and spelling strategies. Other times the mini-lesson becomes a forum for children to tell about the literacy goals they are currently working on. Hearing the goals of others allows children to think about possibilities for future goals for themselves. Often we use mini-lessons as brainstorming sessions to generate ideas on various topics: What makes writing *good* writing? What are some ways to find books that you will enjoy? What are effective strategies to use when you proofread your writing?

The possibilities for mini-lessons are endless. Through these short lessons we can address the needs of the moment. I find myself jotting notes about ideas for mini-lessons in my day book.

> *January 11*—Still some confusion between fiction and nonfiction. Need more work on what makes a book nonfiction. Amy, Carl, and Brian could tell about the nonfiction books they are reading for Goals.
> *January 17*—Kids are coming to Communications without their goal sheets. We could use a mini-lesson to remind them of all the things that *need* to be kept in their writing folders.
> *February 8*—Quite a few children have been coming to me recently asking me to write words in their dictionaries that they could easily find elsewhere. Need a "Finding Words" mini-lesson—ask the kids where they locate words to spell (picture dictionaries, charts, homework papers, places they remember seeing the word, etc.).

Notes like these remind me to plan specific mini-lessons. Jane and I discuss other possibilities as we plan for the week. But, more often than not, we find ourselves planning a mini-lesson at the drop of a hat, as a need presents itself.

After a break for gym, music, art, library, or computer instruction, the Communications Workshop resumes with quiet writing in day books. All children and adults write on their chosen topics at this time. The writing possibilities are wide-ranging: short autobiographical entries, continuing fiction stories, research pieces, nonfiction, poems, songs, letters, and lists. At Quiet Writing Time, we all write in our day books. We make the day books out of twenty to thirty pieces of plain white paper enclosed with oak tag covers, bound with a plastic binder. The paper is unlined so that children can format their pages to suit their works of the moment, ruling them with appropriately spaced lines if they desire, and leaving spaces for illustrations where they need them. Again, students work independently at this time. Children use a combination of conventional spelling and sound spelling. They refer to personal dictionaries containing alphabetical lists of commonly used words with extra blank lines on each page. They may request only one word per day be written for them in this dictionary. Beyond that, we will help students to locate words, but we do not allow them to rely on us to spell *for* them. We insist that they practice their spelling strategies and become independent writers.

After about fifteen minutes of quiet writing, I set my own writing aside and begin to wander around to see the writings that the children have done. I talk briefly to them about how they have worked on their goals in the writing. Some of the children return to their work to proofread or to attend to goals they have slighted. As soon as I am up and around, the Quiet Writing Time is officially over, and children may talk quietly as they finish their writing.

After quiet writing, students engage in a variety of literacy pursuits as they continue the writing segment of Communications Workshop. Many students simply continue working in their day books. Others choose from the posters listing *After Day Book Choices* that hang in each room. Possibilities include: Do some writing *outside* of your day book (letters, notes, lists, poems, songs, cards, stories, booklets, etc.); collaborate on a piece with a friend; do research; edit a piece for publication; illustrate a published work; make a poster; read with a friend; read by yourself; listen at the Listening Center. The workshop atmosphere is evident as Communications winds down and children are energetically involved in individual literacy pursuits.

We gather together to end Communications Workshop with a sharing time. At this time students and adults who wish to may read either that day's writing or a selection from a book they have enjoyed during workshop. The sharer chooses one or two listeners to offer their positive comments and questions in response to her work.

End of the Day Question

We reserve the last ten minutes of each day for guided reflection on our day in school. The question for the day is posted on the board. At End of the Day Circle a child reads the question, and those who wish to may respond to it. Some possibilities for questions are:

> What do you value about your work today? What did you do today to help yourself become a better reader? What good thinking did you do in math today? What went well at recess today? What did you do today to help someone else? What will you tell your family about what you did in school today?

We record the children's comments and later transcribe them into the *End of the Day Question Book.* Here is a sample.

> *March 1 What was the best thing that happened at school today?*
> *Bryant:* It was fun and no one got hurt and nothing bad happened to anyone.
> *Erica:* I got two books from the library that I think my mom will like.
> *Thomas:* When I went out to recess Bryant said why don't I play with him. We mixed up his ideas for a game with mine.
> *Susan:* The best thing that happened to me was in the morning I asked Jon if he was my friend, and he said "Yes!"
> *Carter:* I thought of another joke to write in my day book. I've been writing jokes lately.
> *Rebecca:* The best thing that happened was at art, because we got to lay on the rug under the tables and pretend we were Michelangelo.

The children often pick up the *End of the Day Question Book* and peruse it. We value it as a permanent record of reflections on our days at school.

After School

The school day ends as it began. There is short-lived turmoil at the ringing of the bell, when many of the children leave on the first wave of buses. The dismissal excitement gradually eases into calm. The remaining children, packed up and ready to go, help out with classroom chores while they wait for their buses. Someone files the day's Post-its in the class record books. Someone else erases the names on the Choice board. Another child checks who will write out the attendance slips tomorrow and writes these people's names up on the board. We stack chairs and water plants and talk. The children are animated. Now, they are as eager to move on to their after-school pursuits as they were enthusiastic about the upcoming day when they came into the room in the morning.

We feel good that our students are as happy when they leave school as they are when they arrive. During the day they have had many opportunities to be "in charge." They have made independent choices and decisions that have influenced their actions and impacted their learning. Making choices has become a matter of course to them. In addition to being actively involved in their education as individuals, the students have been significant members of a working group as well. We are glad to see our children exerting their collective voice in helping to determine curriculum and to create community. Over the years Jane and I have consciously worked at "letting go" in these areas, allowing the children to pick up the guiding reins more and more. Besides giving children more room to breathe, we want to hear their voices more strongly. We want to be members of a group in which everyone's input is valued, a group that works together to make important decisions that affect our learning.

The Teacher's Role *4*

Jane Doan

Penny turns her old red Saab north on the Merritt Parkway, north toward Maine and our families. We are returning from the NCTE International Conference in New York City. The conference title, "Reconstructing Language and Learning for the Twenty-first Century: Connecting with Our Classrooms," had piqued our interest last winter and we had decided to attend. The idea of an international conference was exciting, and New York City was not too far away. Now, after three days of workshops and a lot of walking through Greenwich Village, we are ready to be home. We had survived our subway ride to Grand Central Station and we had figured out which train to take to get us to Greenwich, Connecticut, where we had left our car. Now as we drove we could reflect on the conference.

"Denny Taylor and David Dillon were so impressive," I say excitedly as we pull out into the northbound traffic. "Their title, 'The Profound Confusion of Teaching and Learning,' just about says it all for me. Teaching *is* a confusing profession. We are always being bombarded with ideas about how to teach and how to improve our classrooms, and with statistics about what this or that test score shows. And just working with children is confusing. They are all so different. I'm never sure how to meet all their needs. I admit to being confused as to what my role is in the classroom. I'm truly confused as to what makes a great educational experience for every child."

"Perhaps that's what the teacher's role is—to stay confused," Penny calmly replies. "Once teachers stop being confused and start believing they *know* how to teach, they will stop being learners. And I believe that it is in our confused role of learner that we are the best teachers."

"Yeah," I agree. "I must be a great teacher, because I am confused all the time. The kids all know that I am always learning something."

"Well, then you are the perfect teacher role model. You always said you wanted to be a model," Penny deadpans.

"Mmmm. Sure, but I meant with blue eyes, blond hair, and long legs."

We sit quietly for a few miles, reflecting on the conference and enjoying the fact that we are on our way home. Our shared silence is comfortable, relaxed, as we sort out all we've learned the past three days.

"Seriously, though, Dillon and Taylor really spoke to me. They were the best reason to attend this conference," I continue. "Dillon's assertion that we suffer from an epidemic of teaching from behind the teacher's head and that we must begin to see through the eyes of the children makes sense to me. Too often I am making decisions from my perspective, from what I feel would work from my personal experience without considering what would work from the children's perspective. I need to work harder to see through the children's eyes."

"Now, Jane, you need to look at what we do a little more closely. I believe that we do try to get away from teaching from behind our heads. We do try to involve the children in our decision making. We do help them to take responsibility for their own learning."

"Yes, we do a lot," I reply. "But there is more that we can do—I just know it. Dillon and Taylor got me thinking. How about if next year we . . ."

The ideas are flowing so rapidly by the time we get to Hartford that we miss our turn and add an extra hour of driving time to our trip. More time to discuss. In fact, the long discussion of possible changes we can make, areas we can strengthen, and ideas that we will continue to use as part of our multiage program makes the seven-hour trip fly by.

Penny and I are lucky. We have each other to use as sounding boards to bounce our questions and ideas off of. It is this support for risk taking and learning that keeps our multiage program from becoming static—that keeps us growing as learners. Coteaching has become a way of life for us. We do not know how we would fare if we were to teach alone again. We do know that we do not want to. In our discussion of the teacher's role in a student choice program it is impossible for us to talk about what we do without talking about coteaching. We understand that not everyone is so fortunate as to be able to coteach. We also understand that all teachers can have a professional friend who shares their educational philosophy and can work as their sounding board. In this chapter as I refer to how Penny and I coteach, it is with the knowledge that all of us learn best when we are able to mull over and question our discoveries with a friend.

Coteaching is not like team teaching. For example, I do not work in the area of literacy while Penny handles math and science. We both teach all academic and social areas. We often teach together, modeling for the children how to collaborate. Sometimes we work separately, each with a group of children in our own rooms. Other times one of us might teach while the other observes, researching and evaluating what is happening for our children. Always, though, there is communication going on between us. We are questioning what we are doing, why we are doing it, and whom the activity is for—the children, an administrator, or us.

A typical day would look somewhat like this.

7:20

I arrive at school, unlock the classroom doors, and check the day's plans to make sure I have all my materials. I frantically search everywhere for the form that has to be turned in to the office today requesting a bus for our next field trip.

7:30

Penny arrives and I immediately corner her to discuss just how the Investigations Workshop will go today and where the field trip form is. Penny always knows. Another reason to coteach.

8:00

The first children arrive, sign up for Choice Time and help us get ready for the day. Penny and I meet in the Little Room between our two rooms to discuss a new idea Penny has for Investigations Time. "Let's put them into groups of four with a facilitator, and each group can think of ideas for the Little Room. Then we can all get together in your room and vote on what the Little Room should become. This way might generate more varied ideas than if we just all meet in your room and make suggestions as we planned."

"Great," I agree, and move back to my room to be shown Georgianna's new shoes.

8:20

Talking Journal begins. The children and teachers are in their own "homeroom," either Room 105 or Room 106. A child brings me a note from Penny reminding me that we will need more time this morning at Investigations Workshop to allow for the small groups to discuss what they would like to do in the Little Room for Dramatic Play during our current ocean theme.

8:45

Morning Meeting. All the children are in Room 105. Today I work with the children on literacy activities. I keep an eye on the clock so I will finish on time for a change. Penny observes along with one child. They share their observations at the close of Morning Meeting. Tomorrow Penny and I will reverse our roles.

9:15

Choice Time. Penny and I are in our respective rooms, each working with two children on their goal conferences. The children are in whichever room they chose.

9:45

Investigations Workshop. Again we all gather together in Room 105. Penny leads a short discussion about the Little Room and on how to work in groups, organizes the groups, and sends them off to find a spot in either room to work. Penny and I help where needed, but mostly we stay out of the children's way as they think and plan. When everyone returns to my room, the facilitators offer each group's ideas for what they would like the Little Room to be. Penny records them on a chart while I observe, taking note of good listening, good questions, and great defenses of each plan. Once the vote is taken, the children choose the props they wish to make and divide into groups to do the work. Some move into Room 106, while others remain in Room 105. Penny and I again monitor the groups, helping, suggesting, explaining.

10:30

Recess. Penny and I discuss how the morning has gone so far. We reflect on how Timmy participated today during Morning Meeting and share our insights as to why Doug was so distracted during the same time. I suggest that perhaps the children need to have more opportunities for ownership during the Morning Meeting. Penny replies that perhaps the children could take turns leading parts of the meeting, just as they lead Talking Journal.

"It is their meeting," she insists. "They should be able to choose the poem we will share and to lead the reading of it."

"A good start," I agree. "At Communications Workshop, let's ask for a volunteer to choose the poem for tomorrow and to copy it onto a chart."

10:50

The children go to their developmental math group. One group works with Penny in Room 106. The others are with me in Room 105.

11:30

The children get ready for Communications Workshop. They take their writing supplies to the room they have chosen to work in at Communications for the next two weeks and select their reading materials. They choose where they will sit and place all their books and materials there. Then they return to their homeroom to get ready for lunch.

11:40

Lunch. We take the children to the cafeteria, pick up our lunches, and return to Room 106. Over lunch we worry about our math program. I push for more of a workshop atmosphere, with the children choosing their math activities. The standardized achievement tests coming up next month seem to immobilize us. All the children must cover the material that will be on the test. They have no choice. "Or do they?" we wonder. How can we give them more choice in math? It's a question not answered in a twenty-minute lunch period.

12:00

We pick the children up from the cafeteria and all return to Room 105. Penny reads a story while I observe, except for the moments when I get caught up in the story, too.

12:20

Communications Workshop. Quiet Reading, followed by Reading with a Friend. The children are in their chosen room. Penny and I are in our homerooms doing what I enjoy best—reading.

12:50

Mini-Lesson. All the children are in Room 105, where Penny and I model how to help a friend use more details in her writing. I read my latest story about my cat, Sugar Pie, Honey Bunch. Penny questions me about what Sugar Pie is doing in the story, where she is, how high she jumps, and what made the crash. Her questions show the children and me that I have left out details necessary to the reader's understanding of the story.

1:00

Specials. Penny's children go to gym and my children go to art. We use the next forty-five minutes to plan for the next week and to continue our math worries. We decide on trying a math workshop one day a week.

1:45

Communications Workshop, writing portion. Penny and I, each in our homeroom, write during our Quiet Writing Time. Then we conference with some children. Other children peer-conference. I notice that Joanna is using questions similar to Penny's in responding to Alicia's story. Someone heard our mini-lesson. Sharing time ends the Communications Workshop.

2:30

The children gather in their homerooms for End of the Day Circle. One child reads the question for today: "What good thinking did you do today?" I call on several children and jot down their comments to post later in the *End of the Day Question Book.*

2:45

The children get ready to go home. Bus dismissal begins. Those children on later buses help to clean up the classroom and get it ready for tomorrow. I begin to write tomorrow's Morning Message on chart paper.

3:10

The last child has left and Penny and I sit in her room to reflect on the day. Penny questions End of the Day Circle. "Wouldn't it be better if the children took turns running it and we just had to record what they say?"

"Yes!" I reply. "Why didn't I think of that? It's another way they can have responsibility for what is going on at school. And I bet they will do it better than I do."

We spend the next hour and a half doing what I call "school chores": washing off the tables, searching for my plan book, changing the Choice board, writing up a new End of the Day Question, writing in the *End of the Day Question Book,* taking down a bulletin board, deciding on books to use with Literature Groups, searching for the clay, calling parents, and talking and joking with the other teachers in our school. While we are doing all these things, Penny and I are constantly running in and out of each other's room as different ideas occur to us. In this rather haphazard way we manage to review the day, note children's achievements and concerns, brainstorm ideas on how to help individuals, and assess our multiage program in general. The *Why?* question, the *Whom is this really for?* question, and the *How?* question keep us thinking and planning even as we do our normal school chores.

4:40

Time to go home. Another school day is over.

7:20

That night, I call Penny to discuss some more ideas for Math Workshop. We agree that a workshop format in math will help ease our math worries.

Our day is filled with the sharing of ideas, observations, and concerns. Through our talk we solidify our plans, discover new ideas, and support each other in our risk taking. Our coteaching is a support group of two. It has become our way to improve the educational climate for our children, our way to ensure that we are offering our children a wide variety in their school day, and that we are giving them ownership and responsibility for their learning.

American children's educational achievements are often compared to those of Chinese and Japanese children's, with the American children coming out of the studies on the lower end of the scale. Experts often say that this is because the Asian children attend school for many more hours a day and for more days a year than their American counterparts. But I believe a major positive difference is that Asian teachers do not teach a full day. They spend part of their day, up to a third, working in their offices, discussing and collaborating with other teachers (Stevenson and Stigler 1992, 164).

In America little, if any, time is allowed for teacher collaboration. Teachers do not have their own offices. Often there is no space in the school where one can sit quietly with a colleague and mull over educational philosophy. Yet it is essential that teachers make the time and find the place for intellectual conversations. We believe that it is exactly this mulling over, this reflecting on our teaching practices, this ongoing discussion of our classroom routines, this casual evaluation of our children's work that helps us to maintain a learning environment that encourages choice.

In order to organize a rich learning environment that encourages choice, teachers must first assume the power necessary to ensure that they themselves have choice in developing their classroom procedures. For some, this will mean closing the door and quietly doing their own thing without any fuss or bother. For others this will involve a confrontation with the administration to allow all the teachers in their school the autonomy to teach as each thinks best. For a lucky few, this will be easy because they already have an administration that believes in teacher choice as well as student choice.

Whatever the political situation, teachers cannot allow children autonomy unless and until they experience it themselves. If the teacher is not "in charge," it is impossible for her to share that authority with the children. The first step in developing a classroom of choice is to have choices yourself. We were lucky because at the time we wanted to begin our multiage program, our superintendent wanted to institute parent choice in our district. In order to have parent choice, it is necessary for teachers to have choice in setting up their programs. It follows then that the children will have choice, too.

Once choice becomes a factor in the educational program, there are many ways that a teacher can ensure that children will have choice in the program. First, teachers must rethink their role in the classroom. It is necessary to move away from the traditional role of being the sole dispenser of information. The teacher's role in a classroom of choice is multifaceted. In our multiage program:

- We model classroom procedures.
- We model choice making and learning for the children.
- We share with the children our values and expectations
- We provide a safe environment that encourages risk taking and questioning.
- We talk to the children as people.
- We provide real choices, real situations.
- We act as guides who help the children make their educational choices a positive learning experience, encouraging children to assume ownership of their learning.
- We gather information about our children to help us and them evaluate their learning.
- We involve the children in curriculum planning.
- We allow children the responsibility to solve their own problems.
- We reflect daily on how our educational program meshes with our educational philosophy.
- We involve the parents in our program, supporting the home-school link.
- We provide a quiet, calm atmosphere.
- We provide a physical environment that makes choice easy.

We Model Classroom Procedures

Coteaching provides Penny and me with the opportunity to role-play as we model classroom procedures. Fortunately, Penny is a terrific actor and I am a good sport. The ideas for role-playing mini-lessons come either from our need to demonstrate a new procedure or from observations of the children's behaviors.

At the beginning of the year we always model how we conduct a peer-editing conference. The children sit on the rug. Penny and I sit on chairs facing one another, at the front of the group.

"Penny, I would like you to listen to my story and tell me if I need to add any more details to it," I begin. Then I read aloud my story about Sugar Pie, my cat. Penny listens intently and patiently until I finish. Then she comments. "I really like your topic. I think it is interesting to learn about other people's pets. I like that you told that your cat's name is Sugar Pie, but I would like to know what your cat looks like. Do you think could add that?"

"Sure," I reply. "Did you like the part where I told about how Sugar Pie opens up my bureau drawer and pulls out my socks to play with?" I ask.

Penny laughs. "That part is really funny, but I was wondering how she can reach that drawer. Maybe you could tell us which drawer it is and how she gets to it."

"Mmmm, maybe. Do you think adding that would help my story?"

And on we continue, with Penny giving me several more positive suggestions for improving my writing.

Penny and I have role-played how to share books during Read with a Friend Time, how to put books away properly, how to take good care of the day book, deciding which room to be in at Communications Workshop, helping a friend with sound spelling, and many other of the procedures that take place throughout the school day. Modeling these procedures is fun for both us and the children. These "skits" seem to make a longer-lasting impression on the children than lecturing them on the procedures.

We Model Choice Making and Learning

Often during our teaching day, there comes an opportunity to make a choice about what to do next. It seems that our well-laid lesson plans just never work out the way we thought they would. Most often the problem is one of time. We use these opportunities to model decision making for the children.

Penny is leading the children at Morning Meeting Time. She has just begun the Morning Message part of the meeting when the fire drill bell rings. The children march out of the building in a more or less orderly fashion to our spot on the playground. Penny and I groan as we follow them because we know that this will take at least fifteen minutes away from our time. We still have to do the Morning Message, Choice Time, and Investigations Workshop before our 10:30 recess. The Investigations Workshop planned for today requires at least forty-five minutes. We are already behind schedule due to some very important extra long sharing at the beginning of our Morning Meeting. It's 9:15 already. We never eliminate Choice Time from our morning. That thirty-minute block of time is sacred. What shall we do?

When we are back in the room, again clustered on the rug near the chart stand and calmed down from the excitement a fire drill always brings, Penny looks over at me and asks, "What do you think we should do for the rest of the morning?"

I outline our options aloud. "We could forget about doing the Morning Message. That would give us an extra thirty minutes. But we want to do this message! It tells about our visitor who is coming tomorrow. It's important that the children know about that and we also want the parents to find out about it on the children's homework. We could skip Choice Time, but we have never eliminated Choice Time yet. I don't believe we should start now. Or, we could change our plan for the Investigations Workshop and do tomorrow what we had planned for today. Maybe the children could help us decide what we would do to work on our theme today. What I really think is that we should change Investigations Time."

Penny agrees. "That's what makes the most sense." And we finish the Morning Message.

Following the message, the children have many ideas about how Investigations should go. Penny's question of "Why?" following each suggestion stimulates much thought as each idea is defended by its contributor. It is interesting to hear the children explain their ideas in a manner similar to the one I used to explain my thoughts about the morning's plan. A vote is held and the children decide that they would like to have Penny read another chapter of our theme book, *Farmer Boy* by Laura Ingalls Wilder. It's an idea that we both vote for, too.

Penny and I want our children to be able to make decisions on their own. We try to give them all the tools they will need to do this by modeling how we go about making choices. Coteaching helps when we want to demonstrate to the children how we think through a problem and make a choice. In our coteaching experience there are many opportunities to make a choice. We model scheduling decisions, procedural decisions, choices as to what book to read or what size paper to use. Often, when there is the necessity of making a choice in the classroom (sometimes this seems like it happens all day long) and we are in one room together, we try to model the thinking that leads to our choice. Teaching alone would perhaps mean that I would have to talk out loud to myself on the many occasions I needed to make one choice or another. I would do this, though, because I believe that children have to hear our thought processes in order to have a working model for their decision making.

We Share Our Values and Expectations with the Children

It is important for the children to know who we are—our values and expectations for how people behave in our world. We believe that if the children see us as principled, courteous people, then they will follow our example and share those principles with us. We also feel that the children's knowledge of us as real people helps them to see how to take control of their own social and academic lives.

Individually, we share ourselves with the children during Talking Journal Time, when we share personal news, and at Communications Time, when we share our writing. These parts of our day allow us to demonstrate to the children the parts of our lives that occur outside the classroom. We tell and write of our families, our pets, our trips, our professional work, and our vacations. We fill these stories with the whys and hows of our existence, showing the children how we behave in the world outside the school walls.

Most important, our coteaching makes it easy for us to show the children how we behave toward others. As we interact with each other, we show the children how we value each other, how we trust each other, and how we rely on one another for support, ideas, and fun. The two of us openly communicate in front of the class. We discuss our ideas for curriculum, our plans for the day, our feelings about how a theme is developing, and our thoughts about what help we need from each other. Through these discussions and through all our daily interactions, the children see two adults maintaining a respectful, caring, and supportive relationship.

The children in our program know the small, seemingly unimportant details about us, such as our favorite colors. They know that my favorite animal is the elephant and that Penny likes rabbits. They also know that we dislike violence of any sort and that we rely on other means to settle disagreements. When they see us helping each other, they know that we believe it is our responsibility to lend a hand whenever and wherever there is a need for help.

We want our children to respect and care for each other. We hope they will be nurturing human beings. It is our belief that in order for children to have esteem for others, they must see this behavior modeled by the significant adults in their lives.

We Provide a Safe Environment That Encourages Risk Taking and Questioning

In any classroom, there are so many differences in age, ability, interest, size, etc., that valuing differences seems to be the normal state of affairs. In a multiage classroom there is an even wider range of differences. There also is no norm in a multiage classroom, no reading or math level that everyone is supposed to have attained just because they are in this room. Without "grade level" expectations, it has become easy for the expectation to become that each of us will do our best as learners and thinkers. It has become the common rule that we value and support one another in our role as learners. The children see that Penny and I value each child for the contributions he makes to our community. They follow our example and value one another, creating with us a supportive learning climate.

Jared looks out over the sea of raised hands. His turn at literacy sharing is over and now he is ready to choose the next person who wants to share. Carefully he looks at each child in turn, pondering his decision. Friendship influences his choice as he calls, "Pat." He stands up to go back to his place on the rug. "Pat can share next."

"I want to read from this book, *The Bravest Dog Ever*." Pat announces. "I read it at Choice Time. It is a true story about a real dog. I think everyone will like it. I really do." He proudly continues, "It is the first book that I can really read. "

I hold my breath. Pat is a third-year student who has not believed in himself as a reader. He contributes to all our discussions. In fact, he is our resident scientific expert as far as the children are concerned. But he has not seen himself as a reader. He has never before offered to read to the class. The children wait expectantly. Pat opens his book and begins. He has practiced reading this book at home. It is important to him that he share it. I mentally send him all my good wishes. He comes to a word that he is not sure of. He hesitates. The children smile to show that they support him. His best friend, Jared, moves closer so he can see the words in the book. Then Pat looks to Jared and asks him what the word is. "Anchorage," Jared prompts. That problem solved, he goes on, gaining confidence as he reads.

When he finishes, Julie raises her hand. "I liked the way you read with expression," she remarks. "And you read nice and loud. I could hear you and I'm sitting in the back."

"You picked a wicked awesome story to read," Doug contributes.

"I liked the story," adds Jamie. "It's exciting. Is it really true? Can I read that book next?"

Pat thanks his peers, passes the book to Jamie and sits down. The smile on his face tells me that reading is not going to be so scary to Pat from now on. And I am right. The next day he asks to read again to the class. The children's support has allowed Pat to take the risk of reading in public. He felt safe enough to take this important step in his reading growth.

In order to promote such a safe environment in our classrooms, we work on respect. We respect each child for who he is. We show our respect by listening to the children as they share what is important to them. We show our respect by asking their opinions, by allowing them input into our curricular decisions, by giving them choices of what room to be in, where to sit, what activity to do, what book to read, what story to write, what goal to work on. We write children's contributions to the class on Post-its. These "noticings" are shared aloud with the class and pasted in the class record book for all to read. We value their differences in ability and interests. We share our interests and abilities with the class, demonstrating that we value each other for who we are. The children know that while I love to read, I do not like to write. They are aware of Penny's ability to write and actively seek her out to hear her stories. We call the children by their first names and they call us by ours. We encourage them to see that we are all learners together.

When children feel they are respected, they will respect each other. This mutual respect fosters a very safe environment for risk taking. The children surprise us with how willing they are to take educational risks in front of their peers. I remember my school years. I never felt safe enough to try anything new!

Another day, Penny is reading a poem to the children. One of the words is *careening*. Margo raises her hand to ask what it means. Penny has an explanation, of course, but I have to admit that while I had an inkling as to what it meant, I was not anxious to try to give a definition for it. Penny made the meaning clear for both me and the children. I thank Margo for asking the question. She helped me to be a learner today.

We encourage questions. We model this by asking each other or the children when we do not know something. Mistakes are seen as learning tools. We acknowledge our mistakes and talk about our learning. We model how to use dictionaries and encyclopedias when we are unsure of our knowledge. We show the children that we are not afraid to ask the librarian or other teachers for information we are not certain of.

Throughout the school day, from when the first child arrives in the morning until the last one leaves in the afternoon, we try to show through our attention to their needs that each person is a valued member of our community. Following this modeling, the children come to show us and their peers the courtesy and respect necessary for a comfort level that promotes risk taking.

We Talk to the Children as People

Our choice of language in the classroom, both written and oral, also shows our respect for the children. We communicate with the children as people, using the same language we would use with our peers, never talking down to them or simplifying our language. The children question words they don't understand and soon make them their own.

Matt sat quietly as his Literature Group reviewed the Literature Group goals with Penny. Suddenly he thought of one of the goals. His hand shot up. Penny looked over and called on him, happy that he was participating in their conversation.

"You should ask questions," he stated.

"Why should you ask questions?" asked Penny.

"Well—" Matt stood up tall and proud. He said, "If you didn't know what a word meant you could ask about it." He thought a moment. Then he came up with the longest word he knew. "Like *bibliography*. If you didn't know what *bibliography* meant you should ask and then you would know."

"Do you know what bibliography means?" asked Penny.

"Sure," replied Matt with a smile. "It's a list of the names of books you have used. Like when we did our pet research and wrote a bibliography at the end."

Penny was impressed. We had asked the children to include bibliographies with their pet research, but that was months ago! Matt had listened and learned that word.

We Provide Real Choices, Real Situations

In our program we try to make every choice a real choice for the children. By this I mean that children truly have a choice in that matter. If we tell the children that they can decide on the Investigations Workshop activity for the day and put their suggestions to a vote, then we abide by the results of that vote. If we tell the children that they can choose what books they will read, we do not limit their selection to only a certain few, although we may use goal setting to encourage them to choose from a specific genre for a part of their reading. Once a choice is made, each child takes responsibility for that choice. If a child chooses Big Blocks for Choice Time, than that is the activity he will do for the entire half hour. If a child chooses to work in Room 105 for the next two weeks during Communications Workshop, then Room 105 is where he will be. Once a child has chosen goals for a two-week period, we expect that he will work on these goals.

"Quietly get ready for Communications Workshop. Then come sit on the rug here or on the benches in Penny's room until everyone is ready to go to lunch," I direct. The children get up from their math sharing and go to their cubbies. Math things put away, they get out their writing supplies (day book, writing folder with their personal dictionaries and their literacy goal sheets, and favorite pencils or crayons). Then they move to the room they have chosen to have Communications Workshop in. Once there they peruse the bookshelves, selecting the books they would like to read today. Next they must choose where to sit. Mary looks for her sister Hannah. Of course she wants to sit by her. They always have a great time together.

"Remember your goals as you get ready for Communications Workshop," I remind the class. Mary stops halfway to the table where Hannah is setting up shop. One of her goals is to pick a spot to sit where she will be able to concentrate and do her best work. She has chosen this goal herself, with just a little encouragement from me. Her choice of table partners often leads to less than satisfactory work, both to her and to me. "Where should I sit?" she wonders. "I know that if I sit by Joan I will want to fool around with her, too. Oh, there's Alice. She works hard at her reading and writing. Maybe if I sit by her I will work hard, too." She turns and places her workshop materials next to Alice and hops over to the rug, ready for lunch.

Returning from lunch and story time, Mary regrets her decision. She would much rather sit by either Hannah or Joan. "Jane, just this one time, can I change my place now? I don't want to sit here," she asks.

"Just try it for today. You made your choice," I counter. "I think you made a good choice. You were thinking of your goals. Tomorrow, you will be able to choose again."

Mary sits by Alice. She tries to concentrate on her work and finds that she manages to write more today than she has ever written. Proudly she shares her writing with the class.

The next day, however, Mary is ready to go back to sitting by her sister. This time she sits between Hannah and her friend Joan. At sharing time, Mary has little to show. I mentally note that this is something to talk about at Mary's next conference.

We Act as Guides Who Help the Children Make Their Educational Choices a Positive Learning Experience

Mary comes to her goal-setting conference with her goals, her day book, and a book she has been reading. I begin by asking her if she knows her goals. She begins by telling me about her goal to sit where she can concentrate during Communications Workshop.

"Have you been working on that goal?" I inquire.

"Yes! One day I sat next to Alice," she says proudly. "I did some important writing that day. You remember my Rainbow Story? That's the day I wrote five whole pages full of good details. Alice is really quiet. I could do good thinking when I sat by her."

"I remember," I remark. "How did you feel about your writing that day?"

"Great! I published that book. When I took it home, my mom liked it, too."

"What about the other days since your last conference? Did you remember to work on this goal then?"

"Well, um, I really like to sit by Hannah."

"Does sitting by Hannah help you with your writing?"

"Mmmm, no."

"Are there other times when you could be with Hannah?"

"I could spend Choice Time with her. I usually do—and recess and lunch, and Read with a Friend Time, and sometimes at Math Workshop. I guess I am with Hannah a lot."

"Do you want to keep this as a goal for the next two weeks? Do you want to try it again?"

"Sure. Okay. Let's look at my other writing goal—to put in details. I know I did that. Look at this story . . ."

Our goal-setting conferences are the major way we guide our students in their growth as learners. We try to hold a Goal Conference with each second- and third-year student in our multiage program once every two weeks. Often we do not succeed in this goal of ours, but we stay within a three-week span. During the conference we concentrate on having the child look at what he has been working on and where he needs to go next. We try to keep the goals personal and relevant.

We also use whole-group and small-group situations to help the children focus on what they can do to help themselves to take responsibility for their learning. Morning Messages often refer to developing good work or listening habits. They may discuss how to make an informed choice or what our expectations for one of our workshops are. They may tell the children about the positive learning behaviors we are noticing.

Throughout the school day we help the children to focus on the choices they make as learners. We ask them why they are making the decisions they do. We value their ideas and suggestions for Choice Time and other times of the day. We point out the positive strategies we see them using.

We Gather Information About Our Children to Help Us and Them Evaluate Their Learning

Our day begins and ends with a circle time. In the morning it is Talking Journal, during which the children bring their home into the classroom through their sharing. At this time we take note of the frequency and nature of the children's talk as well as their comments and questions. In the afternoon, during End of the Day Circle, the children reflect on their school day, answering a particular question, such as "How did you help yourself to become a better reader today?" We often construct these questions in response to a need on which we want the children to focus. The questions are posted on the board. The children are aware all day of what we will be asking. During End of the Day Question Time we listen to the children's answers, noticing the types of questions they respond to as well as the thought they put into their responses. Both of these circle times tell us much about each child's ability to express thoughts clearly and audibly as well as each child's willingness to express himself verbally. The information we gain here is shared with the children during a literacy Goal Conference.

At Morning Meeting Time, one of us observes and jots down our noticings of positive behaviors on Post-its. These noticings are shared with the class at the end of the Morning Message and then placed in the class record books, where the child may read them on his own at a later time.

We are able to share the roles of observer and teacher at Story time, too:

> Once again, Penny is reading aloud to the class. Her book for today is *Song and Dance Man*. As soon as Penny finishes reading the book, Ellen immediately raises her hand. "What does *vaudeville* mean?"
>
> "Who has an idea?" queries Penny.
>
> Bill raises his hand. "Vaudeville is what people used to watch before TV was invented. There were jugglers and singers and dancers and all kinds of acts."
>
> Penny looks over to where I am sitting on the rug, enjoying the story and the children's comments. "Write that down!" she directs. I remember my stack of Post-its and that I am supposed to be the observer, and I get busy. I have two new noticings for the class record book. Ellen asked for the definition of a word and Bill explained the meaning of

vaudeville. These are filed in their sections of the book along with all the other noticings that are there.

Investigations, Math, and Communications Workshops also give us insights into each child's strengths and weaknesses. Often the only time to jot these down is after school. Sometimes they only exist in our memories. If they are written down, they too are placed in the class record book. Whether written down or not, all of our observations are shared with the children during Goal Conference.

The children also have portfolios. What they choose to place in their portfolios gives us insight into what they value. Through the portfolios we are able to see how to see what the child believes are his strengths, what he sees as important work.

We use all the information we gather about each child when we meet for a Goal Conference. We use this information to help each child look at what he has been doing, where his successes are, and what he needs to work on. Together we evaluate his learning. This valuing of his work leads to making an informed choice of goals to work on for the next two weeks.

We Involve the Children in Curriculum Planning

While our curriculum is based on our school district's requirements, it revolves around the children's interests and needs. We ask for the children's input at every stage of our curriculum planning. They decide the direction and the focus of our themes. Their interest determines the number of weeks we spend on a theme. They help to plan the speakers, field trips, and other activities involved in a theme study. They feel they are in control, in charge of their learning. They feel ownership.

When we are working with the children to develop a theme, we try, as much as possible, to stay out of the discussions of what we want to learn and how we will accomplish that learning. In addition to our in-class discussions, we often ask the children to write or draw on their homework paper what questions they have on a certain topic or what ideas they have for exploring that topic. Their responses show us where their needs and interests lie. With the children's help, we develop a curriculum that is as child centered as we know how to make it at this time.

We Allow Children the Responsibility to Solve Their Own Problems

Hannah, Mary, and Barbara noisily run into the room at the end of recess. "Joan was bossing us," Mary angrily shouts.

"She wouldn't let us play with Barbara," adds Hannah.

"My feelings are hurt," Barbara sobs.

It's Math time and Math always seems too short. My first inclination is to solve this problem the easy way by telling the girls that I will talk to Joan later. That way, no Math time will be lost. But it's not my problem. It is theirs. And if I make them wait to solve it, it will grow in their minds until no math will be able to fit in.

"You will have to solve this yourselves. Ask Joan to join you in the Little Room and discuss how your recess could have gone better. What choices could you have made differently? Don't come back until you have decided on a plan which will make everyone happy," I direct.

The four girls spend fifteen minutes of Math time working out their differences. They return with a compromise that seems to satisfy them all. Math activities can fill their minds now.

The next day is a repeat performance. The plan seems not to have worked. The four apparently angry girls storm into my room shouting, "We need to go into the Little Room for a discussion." I size up the situation, wondering if they have discovered a way to get out of math. "Five minutes is all you need," I say. "Be back here for math at ten fifty-five." And five minutes later I remind them to come into the classroom. They are all smiling, happy with themselves and their talk. Perhaps just a little too happy, I think.

Wednesday seems to prove my point. Once again the girls come in from recess angrily. This time I tell them that they will have to deal with their problem with me during recess the following day. They have missed enough math dealing with their friendship. The girls' faces fall, but they settle into Math time quickly.

After lunch all four girls bounce into the room together. "We don't need to work out our problem at recess. We sat together at lunch and solved everything!" Proud smiles accompany this announcement. And it appears that they have solved their problem. The next few weeks pass without any recess incidents.

We try never to interfere in situations where the children are able to sort out their difficulties. We provide them with the time and often the space to work things out, whether it is a difficulty in personal relations or in academics. We stay out of the children's way unless we are specifically asked to step in or we believe that intervention is necessary. Always, we evaluate the circumstances and decide if we are really needed. If not, we ask the children to do their own problem solving.

We Reflect Daily on How Our Educational Program Meshes with Our Educational Philosophy

"I just don't know, Penny. I think that I am still too controlling a teacher. I don't give the children enough space to make their own decisions. I am always jumping in with all kinds of advice before the kids have a chance to even think about what they need or want to do. And then they choose to follow my advice rather than think for themselves," I complain as I walk into Penny's room after school.

"What do you mean?" Penny asks, looking up from the table she is wiping.

"Well, I really do believe that the children are able to think and problem-solve for themselves. I know we have modeled that enough for them. I am committed to student choice. But too often I find myself reverting to my old ways. I find it so easy to just tell them what to do, especially if they are having a hard time coming to a decision. I am just awfully quick at taking the child's responsibility and placing it on my shoulders. I guess I just like feeling needed too much."

"I don't see that very often in your interactions with the children," Penny comforts me. "We are going to fall back onto our old ways of teaching sometimes, though. It is important to be aware of it when it happens so we can quickly revise our thinking!"

"Please tell me when you see me doing a 'teacher takeover' that isn't wanted or needed, Penny. I think I need help allowing the children the autonomy necessary for choice making."

"Sure thing. But tell me why you are feeling so controlling today. What opportunities for choice did you deny your kids? Do you really have a concern, or was it just a bad ending to today? Let's talk about what you did today and see how often you interfered with students' choice and how often you promoted it."

We constantly ask what it is that we are doing that can be done by the children instead. "The more we allow the children to do, the more amazed we are at what they can do!" is Penny's constant reminder that children are capable human beings. Continuous evaluation of our class schedule always yields new areas for student choice. Continuous evaluation of our behaviors and strategies in the classroom keeps us aware of our strengths and our weaknesses. A commitment to student choice focuses us on ways to leave teaching from "behind the teacher's head" and to move toward "looking through the children's eyes."

We Involve Parents in Our Program, Supporting the Home-School Link

Parent choice is one of the main reasons that we wanted to start a multiage program in our school district. As a district teacher, I had always had a choice in what classes my children took and which teachers they had. I believe that all parents should be allowed to make these important choices for and with their children. Penny and I also believe that parent involvement in children's education means improved student success.

We strive to help parents to feel that they have a right to be in our classrooms, at any time, with or without prior notice. We encourage them to volunteer on a regular basis if they are able. If regular planned volunteering is not possible, we encourage parents to visit us whenever they can, during a lunch period, or a day off, or whenever. We are always happy to see them. We tell them that they are welcome to call us at home to express concerns or ask questions, or even to tell us what they like about our program, and we back up this talk with our home phone numbers. We ask for their input into their children's educational program, keeping them informed of our current themes and our activities. Parents are a part of our multiage family, members of our educational team.

We Provide a Quiet, Calm Atmosphere

Visitors to our classroom often remark on how calm our classrooms are. They approve of our unruffled voices and see the favorable effect such quietness has on the children. Penny and I both believe that a calm atmosphere encourages the children to be themselves and to be responsible for their learning. A noisy, distressing atmosphere inhibits the ability to think and problem-solve. Discord only causes children to be afraid to take charge, to take risks.

Penny and I naturally speak in quiet tones. Soft voices are just part of our personalities. We cannot take credit for working toward modulating our tones. It's speaking loudly that is difficult for us. But we do see the benefits of using such dulcet tones. We have found that by speaking quietly, we encourage the children to speak quietly.

We tend to take life in stride, remaining calm in most situations. This is also just another aspect of who we are, but again, we find that by projecting a calm outlook, we model this behavior for the children.

We also work hard not to let situations accelerate to the point where we might lose control and need to raise our voices. One help in this area is our use of the planning chair.

Travis sat in the middle of the group at Morning Message Time. He started to play with Alice's long hair. She looked at him and quietly told him she did not like that, and would he please stop. Travis didn't stop, and I decided to intervene. "What is your choice, Travis?" I ask.

"I want to stay here," he replies, looking sheepish.

"What do you need to do, then?" I ask, placing the responsibility for his behavior on his shoulders.

"I will keep my hands to myself," he says, and I go on with the Morning Message.

A few minutes later I notice that Travis is once again bothering Alice by playing with her hair. I tell him, "Travis, you need to find a planning chair and make a plan for how you can return to the group."

Travis slowly walks away from the group by the chart stand, finds a seat at a table by the window, and sits down. For the next five minutes he sits there quietly. I'm not sure if he is thinking of a plan or just enjoying some private time away from us. Then his hand goes up. I go to him and ask what his plan is.

"I will sit away from Alice and look at the message," Travis tells me.

"It sounds like a plan that should work. Come try it," I say and return to the group. Travis returns, too. He sits on the other side of the group from Alice and participates in the rest of Message Time.

When we move to our Choice Time activities, I remark to Travis that I noticed that he had stuck to his plan. He walks to Penny's room knowing that he had chosen to keep his plan and knowing that I knew it, too.

Modeling quiet behavior, gently giving children opportunities to decide how they want to behave, and allowing them ownership of their behavior all help create the calm atmosphere that we feel is important for learning.

We Provide a Physical Environment That Makes Choice Easy

Although in this chapter I have referred to Penny's room or my room, these are just terms to differentiate where the children are. They are our rooms. All of us in our community of learners feel ownership of them.

In our classrooms the materials that we will need to do the work of reading, writing, drawing, and figuring are placed on our shelves within easy reach of everyone. The first two weeks we spend a great deal of time making sure that the children know where to locate everything. We end those two weeks with a scavenger hunt for classroom supplies. In order to complete the hunt, the children need to be aware of our complete inventory of school materials.

We provide the children with the opportunity to choose a space where they can work comfortably. A variety of spaces—small kneeling tables, trapezoid tables, small and large rectangular tables, pillows, and a comfortable rug—offer different types of areas that appeal to differing work needs.

The bulletin boards and the walls of our rooms are decorated with the children's works. The children often design the bulletin boards themselves, choosing to work on these boards at Choice Time.

When the children are making choices, they are aware that they can choose where to do that activity, that the materials they need will be readily available to them, and that they will be working in an environment that belongs to them.

There is, unfortunately, no formula for the perfect teacher. Each person must work within her own belief system to figure out her role in the classroom. Our beliefs about what is important in education, our philosophy of education, direct our behavior. We believe firmly in the value of student choice. We have worked hard to change our role from traditional dictating teacher to member of a democratic classroom. We work hard to maintain that change, to stimulate in the children we work with a sense of ownership over their learning. We work hard at developing in all of us a sense of responsibility for our work. We are far from perfect. But we continue to read and learn and think about ways we can help our children to become autonomous, to take charge of their learning.

Envisioning Curriculum 5

Penelle Chase

"What's our next theme going to be?" Henry asked. He was signing up at the Choice board and had noticed the Clean Up Pet Store choice. During our study of pets we had transformed the Little Room into a pet store. Now that our pets theme was winding down, we needed to get the Little Room emptied out and tidied so that it could "become" something else.

"I know. It's going to be *The Boxcar Children*!" Rebecca announced. "My mom told me, because she read it in the parent letter last week."

"You're right, Rebecca," I said. "We'll be reading *The Boxcar Children* for our theme. I think you guys are going to really like that book. Jane and I both read it when we were kids, and it's still one of our favorites."

We have found, as many teachers have discovered in the last ten years or so, that theme work is a good way to integrate various curricular areas. Our school district has curriculum guidelines in all subject areas. Fortunately, these guidelines are fairly open-ended. There is certain content that we are required to cover, but the methods used to cover it are left to the discretion of the teachers. Because we are given this leeway, we are able to involve our students in directing the learning of the class. Recognizing the children's voices in this important area is another way to strengthen their engagement in their learning.

When Jane and I were planning for the first year of our multiage program, we studied our district's social studies and science guidelines for kindergarten, first, and second grades. We roughed out a three-year cycle of themes that incorporated objectives from the three grade levels. We decided to follow the *What do we know?/What do we want to know?* format that is commonly used in student-centered classrooms.

Some of the themes Jane and I identified as we planned were broad in scope; they included objectives from various content areas, as well as from the different grade levels. *The Boxcar Children* theme is one example of how we use a single theme to encompass portions of different areas of our curriculum. As we read this book by Gertrude Chandler Warner over a six-week period, we integrate objectives from our social studies, science, math, and literacy curricula: basic needs, problem solving, decision making, predicting, shelters, tools, simple machines, environmental issues, social responsibility, and family concerns.

Other themes are more straightforward. For instance, the space theme includes objectives from the astronomy guidelines in our science curriculum over the three-year grade level span. The nine objectives at the kindergarten level range from acknowledging that the sun is a star to naming characteristics of the four seasons. The four objectives at the first-grade level focus on our solar system and the movement of the earth within the solar system. At the second-grade level four objectives center on the importance of Earth's relationship to the sun. We can easily cover these objectives, and many more in related areas, within the context of the space theme.

We do not consider curriculum content to be sacred. Instead, our object is that our students learn how to learn, that they are inquisitive, and that they want to learn. We do not attempt to "cover" a body of knowledge in a sketchy way. We want our students to be deeply involved in learning things that interest them. The theme work that we do becomes a major focus of our days. Our topics are "big" enough to embody many opportunities for involvement. The children and their families help in gathering resources, in sharing expertise, and in directing our course of study. We find that when children have input into determining how to approach their learning, that learning usually exceeds curricular requirements.

No two theme studies proceed on identical courses, but each one is influenced by the input of the students. We do the space theme every third year. We have done it twice now, and the second time was different from the first. Both times space was a popular theme. Both times the theme study continued longer than expected, because no one was ready for it to end. In this chapter I will use our most recent investigation of space to illustrate how our students become involved in their curriculum. I will describe some of the ways our students contributed their ideas and influenced the course of our study as the theme evolved, progressed, and concluded.

Getting Started on Space

Often we use the morning message to communicate information about our theme to the children and, via the homework, to their parents. On a Monday in late January on the day we began our space theme, we wrote the following message on the chart:

January 30

Dear Children,
　　We'll get st _____ on our Space theme this week.
Today we'll br _____ the things we know about space.
We'll illustrate our ideas and make a display on the b _____
boards in our classrooms.
　　Please think about what you would like to learn about space. Write
a space question on the back of your homework to _____ t.
　　Tomorrow Carter's dad will show us a program about sp _____
in his planetarium. We think it will be really interesting!

Love,

Jane and Penny

This message served three purposes: to anticipate what we would be
doing later at Investigations Workshop, to get the children involved with
their families in thinking about space questions, and to tell them about
the upcoming planetarium event which one of our parents was kindly
providing.

　　We often kick off a theme by brainstorming what we know, or what
we think we know, about the topic. Sometimes we have asked the children to think about what they know about our subject the day before,
and we have asked them to write or draw about *that* information on
their homework papers. This time, since we had anticipated the beginning of our space theme for several days as we wrapped up our previous
theme, we felt the children were ready to get right into it by sharing
their space knowledge.

　　The format for brainstorming varies. Depending on how many extra
adults we have on hand that day, we divide up into that many groups.
The more groups we have, the more opportunities we can all have to
share our ideas. The adult records the ideas on big charts in list form, or
on big mural paper with spaces left for illustrating, or, as in this case, on
individual pieces of drawing paper.

　　Having no extra parents or student teachers on hand on this day, we
divided up into two groups, one group in each classroom. My group sat
in the bench area, and I sat at a little table near them to record their
ideas with marker on large drawing paper of varying colors. We discovered that we already knew a lot about space. The children eagerly shared
their knowledge: "There are nine planets," "Saturn has rings around it,"
and "The sun is really a star" were among the offerings. Shawn was one
of the last to contribute. He told us that the sun goes around the earth.
Okay, I thought, we accept all ideas during brainstorming sessions.
Though I heard a few dissenting murmurs, I started to write Shawn's

statement on his paper. He stopped me: "Wait, or is it the other way around?" We waited while he thought about it. "It's one way or the other," he concluded. We decided to write: *The sun goes around the earth, or the earth goes around the sun.*

The children went off to illustrate their *What We Know About Space* papers. I heard Carter whisper to Bridget as they found a table, "The earth does go around the *sun.*" Bridget nodded in agreement; *she* was convinced. The children knew that uncertainties like this one would be cleared up for everyone as our theme study progressed. We would display our brainstorming papers and consult the board frequently during the course of our research to validate or invalidate our ideas.

That night the children had an assignment. Often we suggest that the children do something "extra" on the back of their homework. This time it was a specific direction: "Write a space question on the back of your homework tonight." We have found that doing some talking at home to generate questions works well. In this way parents and other family members get involved with what the class is doing—usually the questions that come in are good ones that indicate some thinking and discussion has occurred. Children choose what form their "back of the homework" work will take. They may write or draw or dictate to parents.

On Tuesday almost all the children had a question, or several questions, about space on the backs of their homework papers. Gordon wanted to know: How come Saturn and Uranus both have rings? and How come space has no gravity? Lauren wanted to know: How did the planets get there? Curtis questioned: Why are there storms on Jupiter? During Investigations Workshop that day the children wrote their space questions on construction paper rockets and planets and moons and stars, and we put them up on another bulletin board: *Our Questions About Space.* These queries would help us to focus our research later on. They would also influence our choice of Investigations activities during our theme study.

Questions are a major component of every theme. In addition to research-type questions, we also think of questions that we can ask the real experts. We try to get out of the classroom to learn as often as possible; we arrange local trips, sometimes to the workplaces of our children's parents. We always pose questions before we go, even if we are only going on a walking trip on the school grounds. We prepare questions for speakers, too. Many individuals from the community come into the classroom to share their expertise. Often parents, relatives, and friends of the children have knowledge, gifts, and abilities which they graciously share with us as well. The children's space questions coincided conveniently with the planetarium presentation that one of our parents provided. John Meader brought in his portable planetarium, an inflatable "bubble" that he operates as a commercial educational enterprise, Northern Stars Planetarium. This exposure to a knowledgeable astronomer and the tools of his trade served as an excellent kickoff for our study of space. John's presentation combined mythology and astronomy.   The children were intrigued. Our End of the Day Question that day was "What did you learn about the stars today?" The children's responses indicated that John had already answered many of our space questions.

The changing of themes is a busy time. It is a transition time as we adapt our physical space to a different course of study. We "move out" all the accumulated products of our previous theme: the projects we've made, the books and other resources we've collected, the student work we've displayed on walls and bulletin boards. We clear out the Museum, which is a set of shelves in my classroom designated as an exhibit area for theme artifacts that the children bring in from home. We clean up the Little Room, so that we can turn it into something else associated with our new theme. The children help with these jobs, as well as with the tasks we do to get ready for our new theme. *Clean Up Little Room* or *Take Down Mammals Bulletin Board* are choice offerings on the Choice board, and children sign up for them.

Look for Space Books is another choice in the beginning days of our space theme. For every theme we collect many books and other resources to have on hand. We gather related fiction and nonfiction books from the public and school libraries, from our classroom shelves, and from the children's home libraries. The children help at Choice Time by searching for theme-related books in our classrooms. They mark the books they find with little adhesive "dots" of a consistent color. Then the children display these books separately so that they are available for reference throughout the weeks of our theme study.

On Tuesday Lauren and Jennifer worked at Choice Time locating books about space. Ryan joined them on Wednesday. They found many books on our science shelves, where the science books are identified by a red piece of tape on the spines. They also discovered a few space fiction selections on the fiction shelves. I reminded them to check the social studies shelf, too. They were busy putting blue stickers on the ones they had found when our librarian delivered a sizable pile of books she had collected for us. The children put blue stickers on these books, too, and arranged the books on the shelves below our big bulletin board. They made this sign for their display: *Space Books have blue dots on them. They go on this shelf.* Jennifer did the writing, Ryan illustrated with a rocket ship taking off, and Lauren affixed a blue dot sticker to the sign for a sample. Now our resources were ready for use.

This group of children learned as they performed this necessary job. They consulted with each other in reading titles and in deciding if a book qualified as a "space book." They became more familiar with our classroom library. In the process of making decisions and creating their display, they were doing real work. Jane and I make the children responsible for the "work" of preparing for our themes whenever possible.

We find that children learn a great deal through play as well. Another way we broaden the scope of the thematic curriculum is through dramatic play. We are fortunate to have an ideal space that we can set up as an "authentic" environment to go along with our themes. This space is a small connecting room between our two classrooms, oddly shaped, roughly six feet by eight feet, which we call the Little Room. As our theme changes, we decide with the children how we will transform the Little Room into a suitable play area for our new theme. Among other things, the Little Room has been an old-fashioned school, a veterinarians' office, a greenhouse, a boxcar, a cave, a dinosaur museum, and an artists' studio. During both of our space themes it has become a space vehicle. In my day book I describe the process of setting up the Little Room during our most recent space study.

Penny's Daybook   February 4

We set up the Little Room with the children in one fell swoop last Wednesday, an early dismissal day. The Jan. 28 message had been about deciding what the Little Room would become, with directions to make suggestions on the backs of their papers to share with the class. The next day we had a meeting to discuss nominations right after message, and then we voted. There were four ideas: a space shuttle, a space station, the "Star Trek" *Voyager,* and a planet. In the discussion I expressed a concern about the potential for violent play if we created a "Star Trek" ship. No, I was assured, the *Voyager* was an exploring ship, and there would not have to be any violence. Some of the Klingons were good guys now anyway. I was still a little nervous, because I was pretty sure how the vote would go. Though it was not overwhelming, the vote did go in favor of the *Voyager.*

Jane and I have not been particularly happy with some of the goings on in the Little Room lately. The play has gotten a little wild on occasion. We had already planned to be more directive in what went on there during this theme. However, we still wanted to involve the children in setting up the area. As a jumping off point, we wrote this message to the children on January 31: "Tomorrow we will turn the L _____ Room into 'Star Trek' *Voyager.* When space crews g _____ up in our space ship, they will ex _____ the universe. They will also do exp _____ , make discoveries, and record data. What k _____ of equipment do you th _____ we need to make for the *Voyager*?" Several of the children had responded to this question on the backs of their homework. Carter thought we should have "Buttens in the Voyager and Star Treck soots." Erin suggested a console; Jennifer thought lights would be good. Curtis realized we needed "shutols, space suits, air tanks, diliathon crystals, and probs." Instead of writing, Rebecca drew a picture of an astronaut all equipped to communicate her ideas about what should go in the Little Room.

So, to get ready to work in the Little Room we listed on a chart these ideas along with the other suggestions from the backs of homework papers. We then took additional ideas from the group and listed those as well. At this point we divided the group in half. One group worked on creating the Little Room equipment in one classroom, while the other group had their regular Choice Time in the other room. We switched groups after forty-five minutes. Jane and I had gathered lots of paper, old manila folders, cardboard, clear acetate, tape, and markers, and we had a good supply of "junk" in the Constructions basket. We quickly let the children choose jobs from the idea list and go to work. For helpers we had our student teacher, Hannah's mom, and either Jane or me to help on the *Voyager* projects. The children were eager and excited—they created a large variety of materials. Lauren worked on drawing and cutting out planets to put up in the *Voyager* windows. Bryant made a pair of glasses out of acetate, with a rubber band stapled to the ends to hold them on. I helped him quite a bit, suggesting he cut out a dent for the nose and trimming the edges with tape. He has great ideas but he has trouble implementing them. Curtis made an interesting robot arm. There were lots of consoles. Thomas made an oxygen tank with an attached mikelike thing for breathing through. Erica and Jan looked through the dress-ups to find appropriate space clothes—some of their choices were dubious, some okay—they kept asking me, "Should we use this?", and I told them to choose. In an hour and a half the little room was transformed.

Though the space theme was less than a week old, already the children were highly involved. In the next few days many of the children requested time during our Morning Meeting to share something they had brought from home. Our theme coincided with some exciting real-life space events: a Russian cosmonaut joining the shuttle *Discovery* crew and the first United States woman to be put in command of a shuttle run. Many children had brought in newspaper articles about these current events, which we shared at Morning Meeting and displayed in and around the museum. Lauren brought in a huge space poster. She explained that only parts of Neptune, Uranus, and Jupiter were shown because they were too big to fit. Carter came in with a story to tell one day, about how he had met the man who discovered Pluto. He didn't remember much about the occasion, however, being only five months old at the time! Maryann brought in a simulated piece of moon rock, which held a place of honor on the top shelf of the museum. Other children brought in books, posters, mobiles, and other artifacts to be displayed or used during our theme. Our families were coming through again with excellent resources to share.

The children were anxious to play in the newly created *Voyager*. For our previous theme, family histories, the Little Room had been a house. However, the children had not played "house" as we had envisioned. Most often, the play degenerated to "cops and robbers," which is a great game, but impractical in our confined space. Jane and I were reacting to some pretty wild free play in the Little Room, and we wanted to rein things in. Remembering the success of our first space study, when the Little Room became the *Challenger* space shuttle, Jane and I decided to model the *Voyager* activities on that experience. We developed four missions for the children to accomplish in four-member "crews" that blasted off into space every morning at Choice Time. In writing these missions we worked to create a balance of research, fun, and fantasy. We wrote up directions and illustrations for accomplishing the missions on oak tag and hung them inside the *Voyager*.

Mission #1: Make a Space Snack

Caution: There is no gravity, so hold everything down!

1. Use one piece of bread for each crew member.
2. Cut the bread in half. Put it on a plate.
3. Spread peanut butter on one half.
4. Put the halves together and eat your snack.
5. Clean up your mess.

Mission #2: Make a Space Drink

Reminder: Help each other to hold everything down—no gravity!

1. Use two teaspoons of Tang for each crew member.
2. Measure Tang into the container of H_2O.
3. Put the top on the container.
4. Hold the container with two hands and shake 20 times.
5. Pour Tang into cups and drink it.

Mission #3: Discover a Planet

1. Explore the solar system for new planets.
2. Look out the windows of *Voyager*, or go for a short space walk.

3. When you discover a new planet, observe it.

4. Work together to fill out the New Planet Data Sheet.

5. Draw a detailed picture of the new planet.

New Planet Data Sheet

1. Describe the planet's atmosphere.

2. Describe the planet's climate.

3. Describe the terrain of the planet.

4. Describe any existing vegetation.

5. Tell about water or other liquids on the planet.

6. Describe the planet's life forms, if any.

7. Describe the planet's satellites.

8. What will you name this planet?

   Submitted by *Voyager* crew members_____

   Date_____

Mission #4: Moon Photos

1. *Voyager* orbits the moon. The crew members take many photos to take back to Earth for further study.

2. Use chalk and black paper to make a "photograph" of the moon.

3. If you discover a crater or a mountain or a sea, think of a name for it and label it on your photograph.

We then stocked the *Voyager* with supplies needed for the missions, books for research, and a Mission Checklist for record keeping.

Voyager Checklist

Date _____

Names of crew members _____

Check to make sure you have these supplies on board before blastoff.

Tissues _____   Crayons _____

Food _____   Pencils _____

Drink _____   Rulers _____

Star Log _____   Paper _____

Books _____

Check off each mission as you accomplish it.

Mission #1 Accomplished _____

Mission #2 Accomplished _____

Mission #3 Accomplished _____

Mission #4 Accomplished _____

Submit this form to Mission Control when you return to Earth.

We introduced the four missions to the children on Thursday, and the first crew blasted off. For this first round of play in the *Voyager,* Jane and I made up groups of three or four children, wrote the groups on slips of paper, and put the slips in a can for a daily drawing. After everyone had had a turn, *Voyager* would become a choice on the Choice board.

Jennifer, Erica, and Susan were the first crew to blast off at Choice Time. We counted down in unison for them and they were off! Later at Investigations Time we asked them to report on their voyage. They hadn't accomplished much of Missions #3 and #4, but they *had* finished #1 and #2. The girls were uncertain about a few of the terms in Mission #3. What did *terrain* and *satellites* mean again? We reviewed all the questions on the Planet Data Sheet for the group, and I explained that this crew had been our space guinea pigs. The term *guinea pigs* amused the children and prompted a whole new discussion. Finally, after all questions were answered, the crew agreed to finish up their work outside of the *Voyager* at Choice Time the next day. Jane and I wondered to ourselves if we had given the crews too many required jobs to do, without enough time for spontaneous play. But we decided we would go with the missions for a little longer to see how other crews handled the load. Maybe crews would learn from previous crews' experiences that they needed to hustle to finish the missions. We reassured ourselves with the knowledge that the *Voyager* would be available as a choice for more spontaneous play after all the children had had turns to go in as a crew.

We could see the children's interest in the space theme snowballing already. Working together to prepare an appropriate environment for the theme had piqued their interest. Even though we had not had any directed "lessons," we found ourselves surrounded by both fictional lore and factual information. On Friday we wrote a Morning Message to inform the children about the collection of space books with blue dots and to encourage them to peruse them. The next Monday we chose a book about the night sky from this collection, read and discussed it during Morning Meeting, and encouraged children to look at the sky themselves that night and to record their observations on the backs of their homework. The next day at Meeting, many children shared their "back of the homework" notes and drawings, enthusiastic because they had seen some of the same constellations as in our planetarium show.

So far, the things that Jane and I were consciously doing to encourage involvement in the space theme were minimal. Mostly, we were providing the children with easy access to space resources and showing them that we valued their space "work." In any case the aura of space was beginning to permeate the room. *Space Bulletin Board* was a popular choice at Choice Time. The board was filling up with assorted stars and planets. Children discussed their creations as they made them. Lauren told Scott: "This is going to be Jupiter. It's big and here's the storm spot." Rebecca began work on a story in her day book, "Space Girl and Comet Boy," which spawned numerous wild space adventure stories by other children. Many children were choosing nonfiction books about space as goal books. Jane and I often chose blue dot books as read-alouds, and these books were popular independent reading choices as well. Children were doing space-related projects at Choice Time. Cassie stapled three pieces of construction paper together to accommodate her chart of the solar system, and Larry began work on a planet book, a page for each planet. Several children were bringing in research on individual planets done at home, too, which we admired and shared during Morning Meeting. With very little adult direction, children were absorbing space information on their own, both at home and at school.

Space Work

Confident that the classroom environment was stimulating space learning on its own, Jane and I now thought about the Investigations we should set up to augment that learning. We took another look at the children's space questions. Besides various specific questions about individual planets and a few queries about the existence of aliens, there were many questions about the size, contents, and characteristics of the universe: Does space have an end? What does an orbit look like? How many stars are there? How come space has no gravity? How far away is Pluto from the sun? How did the planets get there? Knowing that the concept of space is a huge abstraction in itself, we decided it was time to help the children make some connections to their own place in the universe. We planned to address some of their theoretical questions through a book called *Somewhere in the Universe*. For the next few days during Investigations Workshop, we read and discussed *Somewhere in the Universe*, and then the children created their own books. We had copies of *Somewhere in the Universe* as a big book and as small paperbacks. The big book is a double-text book. Its large print sparsely and simply communicates the main focus of the book: that we live in many different places, increasing in size from a house on a road to an endless universe containing many numbers of solar systems. The smaller print in text elaborates with more details and statistics. We found that this book began to answer some of the children's questions and provided us with additional information as well. We realized that the concept of establishing one's place in the universe was an idea that not all of the children were currently able to grasp, but we took a stab at it with this book.

We wanted to expose the children to some resources for finding out answers to their other good questions, so our next plan was to offer a selection of nonfiction books about space for our next series of literature groups. We had multiple copies of some good resource books: *Moonwalk, Space Shuttle, Seasons,* and *Postcards from the Planets.* Each of these books was packed with information, so we presented them as the Literature Group selections and allowed the children to sign up for their first and second choices. Jane and I then sorted the children out into groups, attempting to give the children one of their choices. Brady and Karen lost out this time. We noted their names so that we would be sure to give them their first choices when we chose lit group books the next time. We prepared Literature Group plans for the four books.

Because we knew our normal schedule would be interrupted by our February break, which was three weeks away, we decided to cut the groups short by one week. That year we held Literature Groups twice a week. We planned for two sessions a week for three weeks instead of for four weeks. I was the leader for the *Seasons* group, and I created plans for the upcoming weeks. I wanted to capitalize on the features of *Seasons* that distinguish it as a nonfiction book.

Literature Group Plans for *Seasons*

Session #1

Review the Literature Group goals. Show table of contents. Talk about what the book will cover. Read book aloud discussing content as we go along. Respond to the book in literature logs. Share logs, if time.

Session #2

Review Literature Group goals. Reread first chapter, "The Sun and the Seasons." Discuss reasons for the occurrence of seasons. Use flashlight and globe to demonstrate. Let children take turns holding globe and "revolving" around sun (held by another child). Show how the tilt of the earth and revolution cause seasons. Talk about the length of our year. Write and draw about why we have seasons in literature logs.

Session #3
Review lit group goals. Divide into pairs to "partner read." Let each pair choose one of the four chapters on the individual seasons. Ask children to use table of contents to locate their chapters. After partner reading, the pairs make a mini-report with pictures and words on drawing paper. Use last 10 minutes for each pair to share their reports with the whole group.

Session #4
Review lit group goals. Give children copies of the book. Point out index in *Seasons* and practice using the index to locate information. Show them the indexes in several other nonfiction books. Review the months of the year and practice saying them in order. Decide which months constitute each season. Let the children work in groups to use the month cards to organize the months under the appropriate season card. Brainstorm possibilities for a project on *Seasons*. List them on a chart, discuss, and vote. Make a list of materials we will need.

Session #5
Work on project.

Session #6
Presentation day. Spend 10 minutes getting organized. Do presentation and be audience for the presentations of the other three groups.

After much discussion about project possibilities, the group finally voted to create their own books about the seasons. Most of the children wanted to try out using a table of contents and an index in the book. We decided that each group member could make an individual book, or that members could partner up to work together on a book.

A couple of weeks before vacation, Ryan came to school with a bulging backpack. He brought his bag into the classroom first thing in the morning. "Guess what's in here!" he quizzed Jane. Three guesses later (An alligator? Your little sister? A dozen snowballs?), he opened his bag and tenderly unpacked a complete play-dough solar system that he had fashioned at home. On his own Ryan had come up with the idea of making play-dough models of the planets in the solar system. His mother and sister had helped him make the dough. He modeled, baked, and painted the planets and sun and brought them in to share. After sharing them at Morning Meeting Time, Ryan set his solar system up as a display in our museum. The children were very impressed!

And so were Jane and I. We were impressed with Ryan's initiative, as well as with his product. We saw that Ryan was deeply engaged in his learning. The class was just finishing up the *Where Do I Live?* books, and we had planned our next focus to be on our own solar system. We decided to use Ryan's idea as a choice for the next Investigations project. Since we had a student teacher we could offer the children three choices, and each of us could choose the activity we wanted to lead. Thankfully, Jane *wanted* to be in charge of the play-dough models group! Our student teacher, Darlene, decided on an activity that she discovered in *Nature Scope,* a guide for educators published by the National Wildlife Federation. This activity required the children to combine research and fantasy to create travel posters to advertise trips to other planets in the solar system. The activity I chose, a solar system song-and-dance routine, came from *Nature Scope,* too. We gathered our materials, presented the three choices in a Morning Message, and the children signed up for their choices. That week we spent three Investigations Workshops working on our projects, and we shared for each other the following Monday. Our sharing times are low-key affairs. We gather in Jane's room, push back the chart stand, move the kneeling table, set up a back row of chairs in a semicircle, and sit on the rug when those chairs are filled up. The stage becomes whatever open area is left over up front.

Darlene's travel poster group had subdivided into four groups, each group researching a planet of their choice. Their mission was to discover some true facts about their planet and to include this information in an ad travel packet to encourage visitors. Darlene had shown the children some travel posters and discussed with them some theories behind effective advertising. The children had collected books from the classroom and the library. Darlene and the more advanced readers helped with the reading, and together the groups created brochures and posters.

Their presentation was fun. Lisa, who is reticent in front of large groups, held the poster the Pluto group had created. Kyla, Andy, and Curtis all spoke their memorized lines, entreating folks to give Pluto a try. The Jupiter group had become very involved in their research, and sharing that was the focus of their presentation. Scott and Ryan had worked together doing research during Communications and Choice Time, and Rebecca brought in three pages of research notes and pictures she had done at home. Ryan helped Cassie, a first-year student, to read her research. The Saturn group, Elizabeth, Erica, and Frances, was a bit disorganized and unsure of their facts. Elizabeth tried valiantly to hold it all together as Erica and Frances held up their elaborate poster and tried to think of what to say. Gordon, Carter, Susan, and Chuck had studied about Mars. They were very involved in connecting their research to their advertising campaign. "Come to Mars! It will be your trip of a lifetime! Is red your favorite color? Yes, you will really like Mars, because it is red everywhere. There's nothing to hurt you there, no living things," Curtis and Susan told us. Chuck held up one side of the poster and Gordon read: "Mars is like a red red rose. You would like it. So . . . COME ON! If you come you might see me and Carter. Mars is half the size of Earth." Their poster was illustrated with comparatively sized Mars and Earth, as well as a landing diagram. The travel ad group left the stage to enthusiastic applause.

My song-and-dance group was next. We had learned the words to our song, "The Planets Go Spinning Around the Sun," and prepared a little dance to go with it. In the process we had learned the order of the planets, as well as investigating the concepts of rotation and revolution. Each of us took the part of either a planet or the sun and made appropriately colored large circular cutouts to affix to our fronts. Our dance required us to do some rotating and some revolving as we sang. In practice we concentrated on remembering to sing as we moved. At sharing time the routine went off well, without anyone getting too silly or being too shy. After our song and dance we displayed our fronts and identified ourselves. A couple of the children also explained how planets rotate and revolve, and our group, too, was applauded spiritedly.

Ryan had consented to be Jane's assistant for the play-dough models group. They had had fun. After researching the planet characteristics, they had worked in threesomes to create solar systems. The planets were authentically painted, and each had a toothpick axis. They labeled the planets and displayed their solar systems in shallow boxes. We all strained to see as the three subgroups showed their projects and told what they had learned about the various planets. As the groups carried their displays to the museum, several children in the audience commented that they would ask to do this project at home.

As it was now mid-February, the presentations of our study group projects were quickly followed by Literature Group presentations on the four books we had been studying. The members of each group had decided on a simple project to do together to share their book with the other groups. Literature Group projects are quick and dirty affairs; we usually spend only a single day to complete the project.

On presentation day, my *Seasons* group all read our books aloud, displaying the indexes we had created. I had worked with Bridget, who did not have a partner and who really wanted one. The children enjoyed doing this project, and the books were well received by the audience. We also enjoyed the presentations of the other groups: the play that the *Moonwalk* group performed, the larger-than-life-size postcards that the *Postcards from the Planets* group had made, and the mural depicting the interior of a spaceship that the *Space Shuttle* group displayed.

We were several weeks into our space theme now, and most of the children had blasted off into space in the *Voyager* during an Investigations Workshop time. Many of them had chosen to play in the *Voyager* by signing up for it as a choice at Choice Time, too. Jane and I were pleased with the good balance of fantasy and academic learning that we were observing in the operations of the space crews. Most crews were able to accomplish the missions and still have time left over for free play during their forty-five-minute space voyage during Investigations. And, although there were no requirements for the astronauts when they played in the *Voyager* at Choice Time, the experience of having done the required missions stimulated them to create missions for themselves. Some Choice Time crews made moon photos, designed space equipment, and created "experiments." Their play was innovative but grounded in realism. We were glad that we had intervened by structuring the initial *Voyager* activities, but we wished that the children had had more input into the process. We decided that for our next theme, we would work with a committee of children to decide on suitable activities for whatever the Little Room became; we would experiment with student-designed structure.

We often find that if we introduce or model an activity, the children will extend it on their own, as they did in the *Voyager*. I experienced similar behavior in my math group. At that time the children worked in developmental groups for math for three or four periods each week. My group was composed of the children who were working at the most abstract level. I had a few second-year students, but most of them were third- or fourth-year students. Second graders in our school are required to take standardized achievement tests every spring. With this test in mind, I decided to design some *Voyager* problems to initiate review of particular concepts and skills.

Voyager Adventure Problems

1. Liftoff is scheduled for 10:00 A.M. It is now 8:00 A.M. Draw pictures of two clocks to show the times. How many hours until liftoff?

2. The crew checks the food supply. There is enough bread and peanut butter, but the Tang supply is low. They need 8 tablespoons of Tang, and there are only 3 tablespoons left in the jar. How many more tablespoons of Tang do they need?

3. The commander checks the oxygen tanks. There are four tanks. One tank is full of oxygen, one tank is ½ full, one tank is ¼ full, and one is ⅓ full. Draw a picture of the tanks and label them.

4. The crew members put on their suits and equipment. Each astronaut wears these things: 1 space suit, 1 helmet, 2 gloves, 2

boots, 1 oxygen tank, 1 microphone, and 1 set of earphones. How many things do they put on in all?

5. Liftoff is two minutes away. How many seconds are left for the crew members to get buckled into their seats?

6. 10, 9, 8, 7, 6, 5, 4, 3, 2, 1, 0 . . . Blastoff! *Voyager* rises into the air. There are 24 primary fuel injectors to lift the ship. There are 12 secondary injectors. How many injectors are there in all?

7. The navigator watches the console and reads the screen as *Voyager* goes higher and higher. Fill in the miles that are missing in this data: 100 * 200 * 300 * _____ * _____ * 600 * 700 *_____ * 900 * _____* 1,100 *   1,200   *   _____   *   1,400   *   1,500 * _____ *   _____*   1,800   *   1,900   * _____ .

8. The commander gives instructions to the crew members through the microphone. The mike is a rectangle. Two sides are 9 cm and the other two sides are 5 cm. Use a ruler to draw a picture of the microphone on the back of this paper.

9. The crew members unbuckle their seat belts when the ship has gone 5,000 miles into space. They float around the cockpit, gathering up tools that were not fastened down before liftoff. The navigator grabs 13 tools. The commander gets 6 tools. How many more tools did the navigator grab than the commander?

10. Draw a picture of *Voyager*. In your picture use 5 triangles, 3 circles, 2 rectangles, and 4 squares.

The children tackled these problems independently or in pairs. The next few days we spent discussing their results and thereby reviewing fractions, measuring, patterns, shapes, etc. The children clamored to write some *Voyager* problems themselves, and I was happy to let them. I typed up the problems they produced and made copies for the group. We had fun solving the group's problems as well. And the children discovered that writing a good problem is as challenging as solving one.

The Research Component

We like to include a research component in our themes. Space study lends itself to research. It is a topic that fascinates most children, and there are many resources available for research. Lots of children were reading and talking about the nonfiction theme books we had gathered early on in our study. We noticed many children doing research on their own as our theme study progressed. Tara came to school with a report she had done at home about Pluto. Erin read Seymour Simon's *Jupiter* for a reading goal and created a poster about the book to display her new knowledge. Robert discovered a wealth of information in his computer's encyclopedia and brought in a new printout every few days.

The children knew that we would be doing a research project to culminate our space theme, and we saw them beginning to gather information on their own. I watched Elizabeth reading *The Magic School Bus Lost in the Solar System* during Communications Workshop one day. I saw her writing some notes on a card that she was using for a bookmark, and I went over to ask her about what she had written. "Oh, I found out in this book about Saturn's rings. They are really lots of those asteroid things. I think I will do my research on Saturn, so I wrote about it here." When I reported this event to Jane, we decided it was time to get started on research projects.

We were intrigued by Elizabeth's natural use of *The Magic School Bus Lost in the Solar System* as a research source. To stimulate more independent research, we decided to offer this book, along with some other nonfiction selections, as an option for the next round of Literature Groups. At our book talk sign-up time the children cheered when we presented this book. As it was obvious to us that any child who did not get to be in the *Magic School Bus* Literature Group would be totally devastated, we suggested doing *Lost in the Solar System* for all the groups.

This suggestion was well received! During the next three lit group sessions we leisurely enjoyed the remarkable adventures of Ms. Frizzle's class, and in the process we learned a lot about our solar system. We spent ten minutes at the end of each session reading and writing in our investigations logs to reflect on what we had learned. It was one of the children who noticed that the "reports" that Ms. Frizzle's students wrote looked similar to the work we did in our logs. They used lined paper with three holes along the side—just the same as the paper in our spiral notebooks! The format for our space research was born. We would do research and write notes in our logs. Then on a clean page we would prepare a final "report," just like Ms. Frizzle's kids.

Doing formal research reports was a new enterprise for some of the children. So far that year our research presentations had taken many forms. Usually, we brainstormed both a list of research topics and a list of ways to present the research. So, making posters, clay models, dioramas, and books or creating speeches, songs, poems, and plays had all been popular project choices. We suspected that writing a report might be a bit challenging for some of the children, so we looked around for some assistance. Jane had noticed an attractive bulletin board about space exploration in an upstairs hallway. She tracked down its creators, a sixth-grade class, and we lucked into some expert helpers.

This Morning Message kicked off the research work:

Dear Children,

We know you have been thinking about possibilities for sp _____ research. Today we will get org _____ to begin our w _____ . We will ch _____ topics and form research groups.

Some sixth grade st _____ will come down to help us with our research during Investigations Workshops this week. We will write our rep _____ and share them next week.

Love,

Penny and Jane

Later that morning at Investigations time, we brainstormed a list of research topics, and we sorted the children into pairs or threesomes to work on topics of their choice. We assigned sixth graders to assist the groups, which were concentrating on topics ranging from *Are spaceships from every country all the same?* to *What is it like on Mars?* to *Are there really aliens?* to *What do astronomers do?* The rest of the week the groups worked during Investigations Time gathering resources, learning how to use indexes, reading, listening, taking notes, and writing and drawing their reports. The sixth graders were invaluable as assistants in accomplishing this work.

The next week during our regular Literature Group meeting time, the children read their reports to their groups. After sharing, the readers asked for questions and comments about their work. Since this is the procedure we follow when we share day books at Communications Workshop, the children are accustomed to receiving this kind of feedback. We hoped that the input from the listeners would help the children in evaluating their own work. After sharing, each child dictated responses to the items on the Project Self-Evaluation sheet, and the lit group leader noted these ideas on the form.

Project Self-Evaluation

Name _____ Date _____

People in my group _____

Name of Project _____

These are some good things about my project:

This is how I could have made my project even better:

We insist that children think about their learning. The project form is open-ended to encourage reflection on successes and possibilities for improvement. Further, the form highlights our expectations: that there will be good work accomplished and that learners should try to do even better work. More mundanely, it also serves as a record of the content of the project and the participants in the group. The self-evaluation forms are stored in the children's portfolios, where they are available for review by children, parents, and teachers.

The reports have been shared, and our theme is winding down. We spend an Investigations Workshop period checking out our original questions. Have we answered them all? Well, we do know that Jupiter is the largest planet, that there is less gravity on the moon than on Earth, that planets move in orbits. We think we understand why we can't feel ourselves moving, even though our planet is revolving and rotating. We have learned that Saturn and Uranus both have rings, that Pluto is very cold and that Mercury is very hot, that we are a very tiny solar system on the edge of a galaxy. We have heard some new words and thought about some new concepts. We haven't come to grips with Rebecca's question: How many stars are there? Or Carter's: Does space have an end? We definitely are not sure about Susan's query: Are there any alien families in space?

Jane and I have mixed feelings. In one sense we all think we know a lot; in another sense we think we have a lot to learn. The classrooms now look comfortably crowded with space stuff: displays, posters, articles, books, murals. It's hard to know if we are ready to move on. "What's next?" Jennifer asks before school as she signs up for *Clean Up Voyager* on the Choice board. And on the window seat Carter holds the globe in his lap and talks to Cassie at his side. "See, here where we are it's winter now, and over here it's summer. You know why, don't you? Because the earth is not straight up and down. It's tilted."

"Where's Hawaii?" Cassie wants to know.

"Here it is," Carter shows her. "It's always summer there."

Hearing interactions like this reassures us. Regardless of the theme, the learning will continue in one form or another.

The Parents' Role ⠀⠀⠀⠀⠀⠀6

Jane Doan

Choosing an Educational Program

Six women sat chatting around the kitchen table. Each was the parent of or more current or former students in our primary multiage class. They volunteered to come together on this snowy day to discuss the role they play as parents in helping their children become self-directed learners. A cup of coffee or tea sat at each person's place, and an array of cookies and pastries covered the table top. In the center of the table was a large tape recorder. This meeting was going to be relaxed and fun. But it was also going to be taped. The following chapter on the parents' role in a multiage classroom is based on the conversations that took place that day.

Marie begins: "I think that the parents' first role when it comes to being involved in their child's education is being aware of the choices of programs there are and making a choice for their children that fits with what they believe. We model being responsible, self-directed learners when we research what the educational possibilities are and then think what best fits our family's needs. I overheard a conversation between my daughter and a friend who was in a single-grade setting. That friend is very unhappy in school. Joanna told her friend, 'When you go to school it doesn't have to be bad. You can like it. Teachers are really nice. Maybe your mom should have checked out the classes some more. I really like school.'

Joanna was familiar with the process we went through before deciding on the multiage class. She understands decision making. She sees it as a way to take responsibility. And she sees it as her parents' job and her job, too."

"I agree," says Kim. "My son William went with me when we were looking at the kindergarten classes and the multiage program. His choice for school was the most structured class we saw. He liked the idea of sitting at his desk, raising his hand, and quietly astounding his teacher with his wisdom. He liked the multiage class, but thought it was too much like preschool, all that playing. He wanted real school. This was one time we overrode his choice. It was important, though, for us to discuss this decision with William, to let him know the reasons for our choice and to let him know we listened to his requests. We put all this input together to make our decision. He felt that he did have some say, even though the final decision wasn't his. He's really happy now that we made the choice we did."

Louise sips her coffee and then adds, "Choosing the educational program we want is *our* responsibility. It's not the school's. We choose their doctor, their dentist, why not their educational program?"

Ella excitedly chimes in: "Yes. It *is* our responsibility. We know our children best. We are the most qualified to make the choice of the right class for them. We shouldn't be willing to just 'take our chances' on this important journey."

These parents are discussing one of the major reasons Penny and I began our multiage program in the public schools. We strongly believe that all parents have the right and responsibility to choose the educational setting that best fits their child's needs. Parents interested in our multiage program are required to visit our classrooms for a morning to see what a typical day might look like. They interact with the children, talking with them about their visions of the program. They spend time discussing our educational philosophy with us. They attend our annual parent informational meeting in the spring, where we present a slide show and a more detailed discussion of our program. Parents also visit the single-grade kindergartens and meet with the teachers there in order to make an informed choice about the educational program they feel best meets their needs and expectations. Once the parents have made a choice, they are free to meet again with us to discuss any lingering questions.

Parents accept their responsibility as educational decision makers, and in doing so demonstrate to their children the importance of making an informed choice. They demonstrate careful research by taking the time to visit and meet with us. They demonstrate careful thinking by weighing the pros and cons of each educational program. By taking the responsibility of educational choice, they prove to their children that making choices is important to them.

Our experience suggests that parents have a variety of reasons for placing their children in a multiage setting. Some choose our program because they want their children to have the choices they see other children making in our class. Some feel there is less pressure on children when they have opportunities to make choices in school. Others like the idea of their child spending three or four years with the same teachers and believe there are many advantages to grouping children of different ages together. Some parents like the idea that in our class it is the norm for children to be unique. Whatever their reasons, the parents, by their choosing, are modeling for their children the kind of thinking we believe is essential in an educated person.

This modeling of decision making and responsibility does not end when the parents have chosen to place their child in the multiage class. Actually, it has just begun. The parents find that they have in fact chosen to play an active role in their child's school life. They have chosen to be active members of their children's educational community.

Becoming a Part of the Multiage Family

The noise level in my room is high. It is May 25, Planting Day, and all the children who will be new to our class in the fall are here to help us plant our pumpkin crop. This is their introduction to the children currently involved in our program, and to Penny and me, their teachers. The current members of our class are helping the new children feel a part of the group. They are showing them around the room and sharing their tales of previous Planting Days.

Meanwhile, in Penny's room, the parents, both new and old, are meeting before we get on the bus to go to Penny's farm. The meeting is necessary for Penny to explain and assign all the various jobs required on this day. But it is even more necessary to introduce the parents of the new members of our class to our multiage family. The more seasoned parents introduce themselves to the newcomers, welcoming and encouraging them. ("We hear the pumpkin patch will be close to the house this year, not out in the back forty like it was last year. We were all exhausted by the time we reached that field. We hardly had enough energy left to plant!") After the short meeting, all the parents join up with their children for the ride to the farm. There we work together, planting seeds and building community.

Throughout the summer the parents will bring their children to the farm for "weeding parties," where the work of caring for our crop and nurturing our community continues. In the fall the parents help with the harvest and the marketing of the pumpkins. They choose to be involved in all areas of this comprehensive class project, and in this way they model involvement for their children.

This concept of involvement in our multiage family does not end with the pumpkin project. Parents volunteer in the classroom, contribute books and materials for all of our themes, act as experts in various activities, and visit our classrooms whenever possible. They take an active interest in every aspect of the program, helping with the daily homework and in general supporting their children as learners.

At our meeting, the conversation continues as the talk turns to the family aspect of the multiage program.

"I like the crossover, too, from home to school and school to home," Ella says. "A lot of times we'll be doing something that just happens to be a family interest and I know they will take it to school because they want to share it. Then, they have learned things at school that became such an interest that it became infectious to the family. It's nice. The reason we have *The Boxcar Children Cookbook* is that they were doing that theme. We had to make recipes like Benny and the others. It kind of goes back and forth like that. It's nice. It makes school not just such a separate entity that, you know, you go there and do your thing and then you're home and you have a whole different life. Instead it's like they kind of just flow into each other."

"That's what a true family is," agrees Kim. "It's one of the main components of the multiage—to create that family caring environment, where it's not teacher and student; it's teachers, parents, and children. You know, there's a big difference when you look at school that way."

The parents value the opportunity to be active partners in their children's education. During the years they are members of our multiage family, they work hard to make certain that the connection from home to school and from school to home remains strong.

Support in Decision Making

Charles looked up from the table where he sat eating his breakfast. "Mom, are you coming to watch my basketball practice today?" he asked. His mom turned around to reply, "No, Charles, remember—I am going to Susan's house to meet with Jane and some other of the multiage parents. We are going to help Jane with the new book."

"Oh, right! Are both Penny and Jane going to be there?" he asked anxiously.

"Mmm. I'm not sure. I think that just Jane will be there. I'm not really sure. Why?"

"Well," Charles began, "if Penny's there, can you ask her something for me? I'm kind of screwed up on my math, my timed math test. I don't know what it is I have to do—or what it really means."

Louise supported Charles through further questioning.

"Have you taken this test yet?"

"No."

"You've talked about it, though?"

"Yep."

"But you're not really sure what you're supposed to be doing with it."

"No."

"What do you think you can do about that?" asked Louise.

"Why, I can ask Penny on Monday. Yeah, that's what I'll do," replied Charles. "Okay. But if you see Penny, you could ask her if it's okay if I ask her about it on Monday."

"Sure I will." Louise smiled.

Later that morning, Louise shares this story about Charles with the group meeting to discuss the parents' role in our multiage class. She chose this story because it had just happened, but also because she believes it demonstrates one of her most important roles as a parent: supporting Charles in his struggle to be responsible for himself.

"I saw his request as self-motivation—what I can do to help myself," she tells us. "He was coming to Mom. First of all he was sharing. He was talking about his problem. Then, after my questions, he was thinking of how he could solve this problem on his own. He knew what he could do, but he still wanted some help from me."

Louise's story shows us one way parents support their children in decision making. She asks her child what he thinks he can do and encourages him to take responsibility, but she also lets him know she is there to help.

Based on responses to a survey question on how parents can help their children make choices, we are able to formulate some important insights into how parents see their role.

First of all, they see helping their children make decisions in a much more global sense than we do. They tell us they start helping their children make choices when they are toddlers, giving them options of playing with this toy or that one. One parent said that life is full of choices, and the sooner children learn to make choices and understand the consequences, the sooner they will learn to make responsible choices. Another suggested that talking with children about the decisions parents make and how and why they are made is a good way to demonstrate the decision-making process. A third parent offered that the best way to help a child learn to make choices is to give the child a part in family decision making—to seriously listen to the child's input and to consider the child's ideas when coming to a conclusion.

Mostly, parents tell us that effective communication is the basis for helping their children learn to make decisions for themselves. Parents say that it is important to explain to children what the choices and their consequences are. They believe that there must be consistently applied boundaries and expectations in order for a child to learn to make responsible choices. They listen to their children's reasoning for making a choice and help them through their thinking process.

Parents also believe that children should know that they do not live in a separate world from adults. Children need to get a realistic picture of life. Adults make choices in their everyday lives, and kids do, too. Parents share their own goals with their children in order to help their children open up to them with their goals.

Parents agree that they must be patient with children. They must give them time to make a choice, to model that it is okay to take time to think about choices. One parent said, "With choice sometimes comes — paralysis." Children must understand that adults sometimes have trouble making choices, too.

One parent talked about the importance of modeling for children how to prioritize choices. She shares with her children how she decides what she will do during the day, placing the most important items on the top of the list. She then asks her children to decide what they will do that day.

As part of our program, all parents work with their child to develop three or four goals their child will work on each school year. These goals are brought to school and later discussed with the children there. At parent conferences we talk about how the work on these goals is progressing.

This goal setting at home leads into our goal setting at school. The parents have shown their children that they are involved with school decisions, and that what their children do at school is important to them.

Helping with Choices at School

It's dismissal time. Robin's mom breathlessly arrives in the classroom to pick her up. It is Thursday. Robin's dance lesson is in half an hour and Joan hates to arrive late. Joan is in a hurry, but Robin has her own agenda. "Look, Mom!" she says. "Look at what I wrote in my day book today. Look at how I used the quotation marks. I'm really getting it. That's one of my goals, you know, to use quotation marks the right way. I think I did it today. What do you think?"

Joan takes a deep breath. She sees how important it is to Robin that she take the time to check over the day's writing. She settles down into one of the chairs and reaches for the day book. "Oh, yes, Robin. You used the quotes before and after the words your character Donna was saying. And, again, down here, you . . ." Their impromptu conference continues for a while. Robin's excitement about her goals is contagious, and Joan visibly relaxes as she talks with her daughter, valuing her work. She knows this time is important to her daughter. Besides, the few minutes this conference takes will not result in their being late for dance class.

Through a survey, we questioned our parents about ways they help their children with academic choices. Most stated that they talk with their children about the school day. They believe that listening supportively to what their children wish to share is one of the best ways they can encourage their children in the academic choices they make. Choice Time activities, writing topics, books read, Literature Groups, Math Workshop choices, and which room the child is working in and why are often topics of home conversation. Parents ask their children what their current literacy goals are and how they are working on them. These goals can often be worked on at home as well as at school during story times or dramatic play that may involve writing. Parents sometimes provide input into their child's literacy goals, suggesting areas their child might wish to work on and helping their child set reasonable goals.

Along with listening, parents suggested that it is important to talk with their children about careers and related learning, to show their children how what they are learning now will play a real and valued part in their future.

Parents also said that they lay the groundwork at home for academic decision making by presenting their children with academic and creative choices. They give them many activities, books, and opportunities to choose from. They read to them from books their children choose. They allow their children a choice of educational television programs.

Providing Experiences

Louise reaches out for another pastry, and takes a deep breath. "You know," she begins, we also help our kids make choices when we support their play at home. That is education, too. You know, little things—like when Patrick was younger and he wanted to play superhero, I gave him a towel to use for a cape, and when he was into castles, I bought him blocks and a castle kit. In his learning I also try to provide materials for him. I support his learning jags just as I support his playing jags. Right now he is on a Gary Paulson jag and I'm helping him find every Paulson book ever written. I'm supporting his choice of reading materials, even though I am also encouraging him to read other authors, too."

"Children have to know that there are so many books to choose from," Alice adds. "I think going to the library is one way we can encourage choices. When they see all those books . . ."

"And bookstores are fun," Marie interjects. Have you been to the new Barnes and Noble store? Just walking in there lets you know that there are tons of authors to choose from. It's almost overwhelming—all those choices. But the kids get to see that there are a lot of interesting books out there."

Kim responds thoughtfully: "Self-motivated learning starts with extending their interests: like going to the firehouse or to the city to see museums. Taking field trips with parents, sort of like Mister Rogers' Picture Show, introduces the child to possible areas of interest. They can choose what they want to continue exploring on their own. Like going to bookstores, these trips show the kids the many ways that they can continue to learn. Someday they will begin to go out on their own. Hopefully they will see these experiences we gave them as a stimulus to initiate their own field trips—to continue to be learners."

Ella adds, "There is a true crossover from school to home, too. They bring home things that are interesting to them. The dinosaur theme became our theme for summer vacation. We took the kids all over New England to visit dinosaur museums and exhibits. It was fun."

Marie muses, "Kim's right, there is a true educational family—not just teacher and students, but teacher, parent, and students. It does make a difference when you look at it that way."

All six parents look thoughtful. A comfortable silence passes as they sip their coffee or tea.

"We support the choices our kids make at school by extending those choices through our home activities. We all are working together," Louise concludes.

The parent survey provided us with many other examples of the ways parents provide experiences that help their children grow as learners. They suggested that it is important to know what themes their children are working on at school and to make materials available to continue that learning at home. Parents felt that if they provided materials for their children at home, then later on the children would see that learning is something that happens at places other than school.

Several parents stated that they feel it is important to find out what their child's current interests are, regardless of what themes are being worked on at school, and to help their child pursue those interests by providing appropriate materials and experiences. They feel that it is important to ask what the child wants to do and allow her to make a choice not only of areas to explore, but of how to explore those areas. The parent's role would be to make available those materials and activities that a child wishes to use in his exploration of a chosen area of interest.

Parents unanimously felt that it is essential for the parent to be a learner, too. The parents can be learning the same topics as the child or be exploring their own interests. It is essential only that the parent model learning. Once again, the important point being that learning is an integral part of life, not just of school.

Modeling

Louise pours herself another cup of coffee and returns to her discussion of Patrick's "learning jags." "One thing that we can model for our children is that a person can go on a learning jag for as long as they want. I share my interests with the children and I discuss that I stay with an interest for as long as I want. There are no limits to what I can learn. And often I come back to something that I already studied, just to refresh my knowledge or maybe because now I am ready to learn more."

"There are so many ways we can model self-directed learning for our children. I mean we have to be learners ourselves," continues Becky. "I suppose, just reading the paper, looking things up. Preparing for Sunday school, sometimes I look things up. Last night when I was reading the paper, there was an article about the space probe *Galileo*. I had no interest in that and hadn't even noticed it. Because they had been talking about *Galileo* at school, Susan spotted it. So we took a look at it and we cut out the article and Susan took it to school. I guess that, in a way, that's modeling."

Louise jumps in. "Exactly, and helping with homework or with their reading and they come upon a word they are not sure of and I even feel unsure how to define that word for them, I will say, 'Hey, let's get the dictionary,' and we look it up. For me, that's modeling how I go about researching something if I'm not sure of it. That's also modeling how to use the dictionary. It helps them to see that they can be responsible for their own learning too, as they become more familiar with research skills."

"Like Tom, he's doing a lot of research on Native American culture," Ella interjects. "He wants to learn to speak Cherokee. So he looked high and low to get a book. He was taking Jimmy everywhere with him because he's home in the afternoon. Finally he ended up getting something through interlibrary loan. I thought that it was good that Jimmy was there, even though he's not actually going to read the book. Jimmy was part of that whole process of how Tom had to dig deeper and deeper to get the information he wanted. Jimmy was part of the process and in addition, he learned a few words of Cherokee!"

Kim leans forward and suggests, "When kids see us continuing to learn, continuing to be interested in new things, then we are being good role models."

Responses to the parent survey support the premise that modeling responsible learning behaviors is one role parents find themselves easily fulfilling. Many parents said that they believe that by being learners themselves who question and make choices they are providing their children with an example that will lead them to become responsible for their own learning.

Parents and other adults do not intrinsically have all the world's knowledge just by virtue of their age, although it might often seem so to children. When parents model the learning process for their children, they definitely are promoting the idea that we are all learners. They are inviting their children to become learners along with them. By demonstrating how they make choices and decisions about their learning, parents help their children to become self-directed learners.

Three of the parents at our meeting have older children who have exited our primary multiage program. They discuss how their older children influence the younger ones.

Ella reflects. "You know, Jimmy is interested in *The Boxcar Children,* which they are reading at school. He wanted the books that Robbie, his older brother, has. He found *The Boxcar Children Cookbook* and had to take it in to school. He is hoping they will be able to make something from that. And Robbie, even though he is no longer in the multiage class, is excited about *The Boxcar Children* again. He is able to support Jimmy's learning."

Becky smiles and looks back from the window, where she has been watching her cat climb up on Jane's snow-covered car. "Older siblings who have been in Jane and Penny's class do play an important role in supporting their younger siblings as learners. It becomes a family affair. Everyone is aware of the thinking and learning going on. The older children provide a continuity. The younger children have a sense of security because they know their older brother or sister was in the program."

"And they survived!" Ella laughs.

"Yes, but more than that, they enrich and extend the learning opportunities the younger child is having because the older child can share his or her experiences, materials, and feelings about them."

"Even the older children can be the models," Louise adds.

"Older children do influence the choices their younger siblings make, just as the materials and opportunities we provide our kids help them learn to make choices and take responsibility for their learning," contributs Kim.

Ella points out, "And our younger children have felt a part of the multiage family since way before they became official members of the class. The first day of school was not scary for them. They already belonged."

Penny and I agree. Both the parents and the older siblings support the children's learning when they are active, self-directed learners. Children want to do as those they love do. They will copy parents' and siblings' behaviors. Demonstrating ownership of one's learning is a positive way for everyone in a family to model self-directed learning.

Volunteering

Another way for parents to act as role models for their children is to volunteer in the classroom. Because we believe that parents are truly an integral part of our multiage family, they are welcome to come into our classrooms at any time. Parents happily take advantage of this open-door policy. They are encouraged to visit whenever they can find the time. We do not ask for prior notification of a visit and we are very careful to involve every parent in whatever classroom activity is happening when they arrive.

Some of our parents are able to volunteer in our classrooms on a regular and scheduled basis. They lead Literature Groups, direct Choice Time activities, help with Investigations and Math Workshops, model reading and writing, and help children to edit and publish their stories and poems. These parents make the time to come at least once a week. Some are professionals who have some control over their daily schedule; some are shift workers or homemakers. We are fortunate that they value their time with the children and that they have the time to give us.

Some parents can visit our class only once in a while. They come in to read to the children or to support them in their Choice Time activities, or just to see what is going on.

Often these parents are able to volunteer to help with special projects. They cook pumpkin recipes or party cookies with a few of the children. They do workshops or talks when we are studying a theme that is in their area of expertise. They help chaperone on field trips, and they sometimes surprise us with a project of their own, such as making ice cream, that is fun for all of us.

Parents who are unable to volunteer during the school day often show their children that they are part of our community by volunteering at home. After their work day they try out pumpkin recipes that are too complicated for us to make at school and then send the results to school with their child for a taste test. They type children's stories, find materials that go along with our themes, find speakers for our class, and support our program in other ways.

Ultimately, all of our parents contribute to our multiage community in some way. They are a part of all we do. Perhaps because they chose to participate in the multiage program from the start, they feel a responsibility to help make the program work. Whatever the reason, we are grateful for our parents' sense of commitment to their children's learning and to our program.

Homework

The parents' sense of commitment is tested every night when they work with their child on his homework. Four nights a week we send home a copy of our Morning Message. Typically this is a one-page message we write on chart paper which we work on together in class. During class time we read the message, decide which words will make sense to put in the blanks, spell those words, and discuss some of the phonics and grammar present in that day's message. We also reproduce the letter on 9" × 12" paper for the children to take home to work on with their parents. Since children are working at different levels, parents participate in the homework assignment in different ways. Depending on the child's facility with reading and writing, the parents' responsibilities range from reading the message out loud to the child and writing the words in the blanks for him as he supplies them, to listening and watching as the child completes the work independently. The children use the homework to show their parents what they know about phonics, writing conventions, and reading. Simply by becoming involved in the homework process, parents can see their child's literacy progress throughout the year. And, since the messages are always pertinent to the goings-on in the classroom, participating in the homework lesson is a good way to stay informed about school activities.

Questioning

Parents also keep on top of what is happening in the classroom by reading our weekly parent newsletter. Through the newsletter they learn about our current theme activities, our field trips, our guest speakers, and our ongoing needs and concerns. Every newsletter ends with the request that parents call us with their questions and concerns.

December 11

Dear Parents,
    We are having some problems telling who belongs to which pair of ski pants. Please help us by labeling your child's clothing. Thanks.
    We will hold our Christmas celebration on Thursday, December twenty-first. On that day we will have an extended Choice Time with seasonal activities. The children will make some cookies for our refreshments. We could use a volunteer or two to come in during Choice Time this week or early next week to help bake the cookies. Let us know if you can help.
    The children in Jane's math class are working on counting money. Jane has asked them to practice at home. If you have any change,

please help them to count it. They are working with pennies, nickels, dimes, and quarters at school.

Once again we want to thank you for taking time to go over the homework with your children. Lately, we have been asking the children to show their parents what they notice on the homework. They are doing a great job of finding the letters in their names, little words inside big ones, root words and endings, the number of sentences on the message, the words they can read, all the vowels on the message and many other wonderful noticings. We are asking the children to share what they have noticed on their homework with the rest of us during Morning Meeting Time. Some of the children have even found things that we haven't noticed! It's great.

Our workbench has become a lonely place this year. There is only one parent volunteer who has been able to come once a week to help with the constructions that happen there. She tells us she can't believe she is volunteering for workbench as she is not a carpenter! But she does wonders with the kids. We hope there is someone else out there who is free and willing to come in during Choice Time (9:15–9:45 Mon. to Thurs., and 8:30–9:00 Fri.). The children love to do workbench as a choice, but they need to have adult supervision.

If you have any questions or comments, please call us.

Sincerely,

Penny and Jane

Another vehicle for parents to let us know about areas of concern is our yearly parent survey, which we send to the parents around the middle of January. On the survey we ask the parents the following three questions:

I am happy about . . .
I am concerned about . . .
I want to know more about . . .

Responses vary, from parents commenting on their pleasure at their child's social, emotional, or academic growth or expressing the comfort they take in our program's family atmosphere, to concerns about invented spelling or questions about what more parents can do at home to help their children.

As the responses come in, we compile the concerns and questions. If many of the parents share the same concern, we use the weekly newsletter to clarify our philosophy in that particular area, or if the situation warrants, we call an informational meeting of the parents. If a particular concern is expressed by only one parent or refers to one child we will request a parent conference as soon as possible.

We generally receive a good response to the survey. The parents see it as one more opportunity to have input into their children's education. They know we value their comments and use their constructive criticism to improve our program.

The most important times for parents' questions are our twice-a-year parent conferences. Fall conferences with our parents begin in mid-October. We schedule conferences at the rate of two or three a week at a time that is convenient for the parents. A thirty- to sixty-minute block of time is allotted for each conference. We want to allow the parents time to feel comfortable enough to ask the hard questions. We have found that after about twenty minutes parents find the confidence to question the "whys" of our program and how specific school experiences can benefit their child. They are able to tell us what they see working for their child, as well as what they see is not working. Together we are able to assess whether their child is moving toward achieving the goals set by both parents and teachers. Together we are able to modify the program, making adjustments that will best contribute to their child's progress. Scheduled spring conferences begin in March. Parents are encouraged to and often do request other conferences when they have immediate concerns.

The three or more years that parents are a part of our multiage family also contributes to the feeling of closeness between the parents and teachers. Parents who have belonged to our community for more than one year feel very comfortable expressing their concerns and questioning our philosophy. They share their ideas and help us to make the changes that will result in providing their child with the best possible learning environment. Parents feel a strong sense of ownership and commitment to the multiage program. It is their program as much as it is ours. They have chosen to be a part of our multiage family.

As the meeting broke up and the cups and saucers were placed in the sink and the leftover cookies and other snacks wrapped up and put away, Louise said, "This was fun. We should meet like this more often. I really enjoyed talking about our kids' education."

Kim smiled. "It is always fun to talk about our children. I think, though, that meeting like this helps us to put in focus our goals and ideas for our children's education. We can think about all the ways we can be a part of their schooling."

I agreed and thanked them for their input. This meeting had been fun. It had given me much of the material that is the basis for this chapter. But more important, it had given me the idea of having a series of small meetings like this where parents would feel free to express themselves. At these meetings we could discuss other ways to involve parents in our program. Parents could share their expectations for their children's educational experiences, and together we could work toward adapting the program to meet these expectations.

The Responsibility of Choice

7

Jane Doan

Goal Setting

As the snow swirled down, the roads in central Maine quickly became slippery and dangerous. Our superintendent decided that it would be best to have an early dismissal so the children could all be home and safe before the storm worsened. Penny and I expected that the children would greet the idea of an early dismissal on a Friday with great joy, but that was not the case.

We heard later that when Susan arrived home she related to her mom, "All the children were disappointed that they had to go home so early." "Were the kids sad to leave because they would miss art?" Becky prodded, aware that the children in Penny's room have art class last thing on Friday afternoon and early dismissal meant no art. It had been two weeks since their last art class because of the Thanksgiving break. It seemed reasonable to Becky that the children would be distressed not to have this favored time once again.

"No!" insisted Susan. "They were disappointed because they didn't want to stop writing. Our writing time was made too short because we had to go home."

Susan's dismay over missed writing time demonstrates the commitment and sense of responsibility children have to their work when they feel that they have some control over their educational choices. During Communications Workshop, Susan has the choice of which room to work in, where to sit, what to write, and which literacy goals to work on. No wonder that a change in the writing portion of the Communications Workshop was distressing to her. She was in charge of her work. She was working hard on the literacy goals she set for herself, and she resented having her working time cut short. She was doing her own important work and was vexed by the weather's rude interruption of it.

15

We began experimenting with self-selected literacy goals several years after we initiated our multiage program. From the start, though, we had been working hard to help the children to be aware of their self-worth at a conscious level by providing them with time to think about their work throughout our day. They used investigations and literature logs to write down their thoughts and ideas. They discussed their reading strategies during our Morning Message. They shared their learning with their peers during mini-lessons at Communications time. The children were used to valuing their learning by reflecting on their day each afternoon and answering our End of the Day Question.

Goal setting was added to our multiage program as a natural extension of those reflections. We see goal setting as a more formal way to concentrate on valuing the learning process and taking ownership of that learning. We see it as a way to encourage children to act as the directors of their own learning. Through goal setting the children have the opportunity to become active participants in their learning, rather than passive receivers of information. They are in charge of their work. They have a role in determining how they will help themselves become better readers and writers. And they have the responsibility to see that they do work toward the goals they set for themselves.

Over the last few years we have modified and refined our goal-setting procedures. Our current process feels comfortable to us as teachers and seems to work well for the children. We know that it will continue to change over the years as we discover new and better ways to help the children help themselves as learners. For now, though, we are very satisfied with what is happening with goal setting in our program.

Children meet with Penny or me once every two weeks to review their literacy goals and to set new ones. These Goal Conferences take place during our Choice Time period while the other children are busy with self-directed Choice activities. During the fifteen-minute conference the children tell how they have been working on the four literacy goals that they had set for themselves. They read to us from a book they have been working on and we do our version of a running record of that reading. Then together we discuss how the reading went, what areas may need working on, what strategies the child used, and what other strategies might have been helpful. We consider how the children have done on their particular goals and talk about possibilities for two new reading goals.

When the two new reading goals are set, we move on to the writing goals. Once again the children describe how they have been working on these goals. They look through their day books, showing their progress in whatever aspect of writing mechanics or style they have chosen to work on. Suggestions for how to improve the writing and ideas for new goals are discussed. Once again the children decide on two writing goals on which they wish to work.

Children learn that they are the ones who decide what they will work on next as they pursue their ultimate goals of becoming even better readers and writers. They learn to believe in themselves as the directors of their learning as they evaluate their development over the past two weeks and set their sights on what they feel are the best possible goals for them to work on in the next two weeks.

Each Goal Conference is unique. Even two successive conferences with the same child will have a different flavor as the child and teacher work together to value the progress made. Our Goal Conference form provides the basic structure, but the children themselves with their individual strengths and needs truly determine the direction of the conference. The next section models a typical goal-setting conference.

"Where are we going to sit for our conference?" asks Charles, balancing his writing folder with his goal sheets, his day book, and a book to read to me.

"Find us a quiet place. I'll be there in a minute," I tell him as I turn to remind Adam and Sam to keep the blocks within the marked block area and ask Alexandra and Lucy if they will keep the game they are getting out to play outside of the block area.

With the boundary issue settled, I follow Charles and Phyllis, who has already joined him, to the table by the window.

"I like this spot," I tell them. "I can see what is going on in the rest of the room, yet this corner spot will give us some privacy, too. Thanks for choosing it. Who would like to start?"

"Me!" says Charles, as he begins to open his writing folder.

"Wait, can you tell me what reading goals you have been working on without looking at them?" I ask, checking if he really has been working on these goals. Charles quickly tells me of the reading strategy he has been working on ("When I see a word I don't know, I will read on to the end of the sentence, then go back and see what word would make sense."). He shows me the book he had selected last time as his goal book. "I have read all of *Hungry, Hungry Sharks*. I really liked the part where it tells about how the sharks eat things that are not food, like fur coats and nails. That is so funny! I learned a lot about sharks, too. Did you know that baby sharks are called *pups*? Do you know that this book is true? It's a nonfiction book."

He goes on telling me more about the story until I interrupt and ask him if he would like to read some of it to me. He does, selecting the part he was most excited about. I do a modified running record as he reads. After three pages, I stop him and ask him to tell me what reading strategies he has been using. When he mentions the one that is his goal, I ask him to tell me more about how that one works.

"Well, here in this sentence, I didn't know what this word, *teeth*, was. So, I remembered my goal and I read on to the end of the sentence. I saw the words *big and sharp*. Then I went back and read the sentence again. I thought hard about what would make sense where I didn't know the word and, just like that, it came to me. It was magic."

"Have you used this strategy in your other reading?" I ask.

"Well, some of the time. But it doesn't always work for me. I use other strategies, too. Sometimes I sound out the word and that works, and sometimes, if I am in a hurry, I just ask Mark and he tells me. He knows all the words, but I am getting better. When I try to think about what would make sense, I usually can read the words, too."

"It seems to me that you have been working hard on your reading goals. Look at what I noticed about what you read. You used other strategies besides the ones you mentioned. I noticed that you used the picture to give you a clue to the word *crab*. And with this word, *kinds,* you went back to where you had seen it before to see if that sentence would help you to remember it. What I liked best is that all through your reading you made sure that what you were reading made sense. You have been reading a lot of books from our science shelves lately. Have you thought about trying some other genre, like poetry, or some fiction, maybe some mysteries or some of our science fiction?"

Charles looks thoughtful. Then he decides. "There are so many books on science. I just want to read some more of them. I will try something else another week. Right now, I want another science book for a goal book. I'd like to read this one, *Rock Collecting*. My brother has a rock collection and I want one, too."

"Fine." I acquiesce. But I can't leave this subject without suggesting that perhaps Charles would like to read some fiction, too, at our Read with a Friend Time.

"Do you have any ideas for another reading goal?" I ask.

"I do!" he exclaims. "I want to tape myself reading *Hungry, Hungry Sharks*. I think I'm ready to do that."

"Me, too," I agree. "Let's write these goals down and move on to your writing."

Charles picks up his day book and looks concerned. "I didn't get to do one of my goals. I just didn't get it done." He apologizes.

"What goal is that?" I gently ask.

"Well, um, I said that I would write a long story to edit and publish and I didn't."

"Let's think about why you didn't get this goal done. What have you been writing?" I prod.

Charles looks up and smiles. "I just had to write about Sam coming over to play with me the other day. We had a great time. And yesterday I wrote about Keith and me going sliding. That was awesome! I did start my long story, 'Charles, the Great,' but I didn't finish it because I had these other things I wanted to write about."

"Do you want to finish that story?" I ask.

"Yes! Charles the Great is the best detective ever. In my story he is looking into the mystery of the missing shark pup. I use some of the stuff I learned about in *Hungry, Hungry Sharks* in my story. So far, the pup has been taken from the aquarium and Charles the Great is looking for him."

"Well, your story has an interesting problem. Have you thought about the solution? Do you want one of your writing goals to be that you will finish this story, and edit and publish it?"

"Sure!" Charles enthusiastically shouts. "I know just what will happen next."

"Whoa," I laugh. "I'd like to be surprised by your solution when you read the story to me. Let's look at your day book now and see how you have been working on your other goal."

"Well," Charles begins. "I was working on putting a lot of details in my writing and look at all the details I put in my story about Kevin and me sliding down the hill. I told where the hill is, what kind of sled I have, who went first, and how silly Keith looked when his sled tipped over on the snow bank and he was all covered with snow. He looked like a snowman."

I read over Charles's work, and I have to agree that he has put quite a lot of effort into adding details to his writing. A few weeks ago, Charles would have just stated that he and Keith had gone sledding and that it was fun. Now he has written an interesting description of their outing.

"What would you like to work on now to help yourself improve as a writer?" I ask.

Charles deliberates. "One thing I need to work on is spelling. Maybe I will make using my dictionary one of my goals. But I do try to do that, and I try to sound-spell. I guess I am working on spelling on my own. Maybe what I could do is work on using interesting words in my story, like Penny showed us in the mini-lesson yesterday. Yes, that's it. I will work on using interesting words in my story."

"Great." I respond as I write down Charles's last goal. "Now can you tell me what the date of our next Goal Conference will be?"

Charles looks at the conference sheet and figures out what the date will be two weeks from now. "February 16! That's two days after Valentine's Day. I know I'll be able to remember that date!"

Our Goal Conference over, Charles spends the rest of Choice Time reading his new goal book, and I turn to Phyllis to begin her conference.

One advantage for teachers in having goal-setting conferences is that the record keeping is built in. All of the comments about the child's work on his goals are written directly on the form. Our running record of the student's reading is kept on the back of the form. The student keeps his Goal Conference Sheets stapled together in his writing folder where they are handy for him to peruse.

When we finished the goal conference, Charles had both old and new Goal Conference Sheets (see Figures 7–1 and 7–2). On the back of this sheet would be the notes I took while Charles was reading a few pages of his goal book to me (Figure 7–3).

Not all of our Goal Conferences are as successful as Charles's. In some instances, a child will not have worked on her goals, and sometimes the child has difficulty thinking of what goals she needs to work on. Sometimes a child may choose goals that are too easy and needs to be nudged toward more appropriate goals.

Penny recently wrote about a difficult goal-setting conference in her day book.

Yesterday I worked with Margo. Her Goals Conference was less than satisfactory in some ways. She couldn't remember her goals, which surprised me. I think of her as being so conscientious. Actually, she had done some work toward her goals, even though she could not remember them. She had read *Rain Drop Splash*. She had not read it on tape, however. When she read it to me, she did not read that well. Obviously, she had not worked on the book. She had read one poetry book, *Play Day*, which is a simple picture book. Her goals had stated that she would read some poetry books. She had not edited her dinosaur stories and written them on a chart. She had been looking up words in her dictionary. In our discussion, we didn't find anything really wrong with the goals—she just hadn't done them. She needed to assert herself a bit more on some of them, i.e., bug me to get chart paper ready, ask for the tape player and a tape, etc. I talked to her about how she needed to take the initiative sometimes. Perhaps this is something we need to remind all the kids to do—remind them that they are in charge. Margo has trouble setting goals for herself, too. She just sort of sits and waits for me to suggest things. She decided to keep her taping goal and to read more poetry books (she picked some out). She also decided to write her story on the chart (we edited it together), and to put lots of details in her writing (I suggested that she go and choose a goal from the Good Writing chart). I will be curious to see if she knows her goals and has been working on them when we meet again.

Communication Workshop Goals

Name *Charles*

Today's date: *January 19*   Date of Goal Review: *February 2*

Goal #1

I will read <u>Hungry, Hungry Sharks.</u>

Charles was able to give an extensive summary of the story. He told his favorite parts and many of the facts he found interesting in the book. He read the selection well, using many reading strategies.

Goal # 2

When I see a word I don't know, I will read on to the end of the sentence, then go back and see what word would make sense.

He used this strategy as well as others. He stated that this strategy does not work all the time, but when it does, it is "like magic."

Goal #3

I will put a lot of details in my writing.

Charles has definitely worked on this goal. He did a very nice job of putting lots of details in his story about sliding with Keith.

Goal #4

I will write a long story to edit and publish.

Not yet, but he has started the story. He would like to keep this goal for next time and finish his story.

Figure 7–1

Communication Workshop Goals

Name *Charles*

Today's date: *February 2*   Date of Goal Review: *February* 16

Goal #1

I will read <u>Rock Collecting</u>.

Goal #2

I will tape myself reading <u>Hungry, Hungry Sharks</u>.

Goal # 3

I will finish my story, <u>Charles the Great</u>, and edit and publish it.

Goal # 4

I will use interesting words in my writing.

Figure 7–2

Hungry Hungry Sharks pp. 28 - 42

hummerhead	Jij	sit	
hammerhead/SC	jewels/SC	suit/SC	group/SC

Charles read well, without hesitation. He used the strategy of reading on, then going back to figure out the word 'group'. (p32). He read for meaning, questioning "hummerhead" (p30) immediately and using the picture for a clue to the word when he read the next sentence, "It is easy to see how it got its name." He also self corrected 'jewels' and 'suit'(p39)using meaning and picture clues . He summarized the story well.

Figure 7–3

We watch the children grow through their Goal Conferences. They move from being dependent on us to suggest goals from which to choose to being able to decide on and write their own. Sometimes the growth is very slow, and at other times we are amazed by the rapid change in a child's ability to be autonomous.

We begin goal setting each year slowly, with the children, as a group, choosing daily reading and writing goals on which everyone in the class will focus. The children will suggest three or four goals as possibilities, and the class then votes on the one they will concentrate on for that day. These group goals introduce the younger children to the idea of goal setting and also remind the more experienced students what goal setting is all about. Asking the children to suggest goals to vote on each day gets them thinking about goal possibilities. After two or three weeks we begin the individual Goal Conferences. By that time the children are accustomed to selecting and working on literacy goals. They quickly suggest goals that are appropriate for them to be working on.

We try to have a balance between the reading and writing goals and between goals referring to mechanics and those referring to style. In our conferences we encourage the children to select goals that are appropriate for them. If we feel a child is suggesting goals that she has already accomplished, we will discuss this with her and perhaps suggest goals that better fit her current learning needs. If a child suggests a goal that we believe is out of her reach at this time, we will also discuss this and suggest more suitable goals. If the child is firm in wanting a goal we believe is too difficult for success, we will allow her to have that as a goal. Often we are surprised by the child's success. Later, if the goal is not completed, we talk about why it was difficult and suggest that while we can save that goal for another time, it is all right to abandon it now.

Through goal setting, the children become aware of their strengths and of their weaknesses. They take the responsibility to work on the areas where they have the most need. And they truly understand that they are in charge of their own learning.

What follows is a list of a few of the goals children have suggested.

Reading strategies

- I will skip over words I don't know and go back to them after I read the rest of the sentence.
- I will point to each word as I read.
- I will think about what makes sense when I read.

Reading materials

- I will practice reading *Snap!* with my book buddy.
- I will choose a nonfiction book to read.
- I will choose a book from the poetry shelf.

Mechanics of writing

- I will put spaces between my words.
- I will use capital letters where they belong.
- I will use periods and other punctuation correctly.

Writing style

- I will put lots of details in my writing.
- I will put some conversation in my story.
- I will try to put feelings in my writing.

Work habits

- I will not sit next to _____ at Communications.
- I will try to write at least three sentences in my day book each day.
- I will use my dictionary more to spell common words.
- I will work hard on my sound spelling.
- I will tape myself reading _____ for my portfolio.

Goal setting is frequently a topic for our literacy mini-lessons. We often spend a mini-lesson asking the children as a class to suggest reading and writing goal possibilities. Penny or I write these ideas down on large chart paper. These charts hang in each of our classrooms and the children refer to them often as they search for new goals to work on. Other mini-lessons may focus on just one aspect of good writing that we wish to bring to the children's attention. Some mini-lessons might be about reading strategies or reading genres. These mini-lessons are often run by those children who have demonstrated that they are comfortable using these particular mechanical structures, stylistic features, or reading strategies.

At least once a month we all sit in a circle and each of us shares one of our goals and tells why we chose that goal or how we are working on it. One purpose of this sharing is to acquaint the children with possibilities for goals that they might not have thought of. Another purpose is to indirectly point out to the children that since they have chosen the goals, they should have real reasons for having chosen them. We want the children to experience the control that they have over their learning.

Penny took some notes at one of our goal sharing sessions last March. We had the children share one of their literacy goals and then tell why they had chosen that goal to work on. Why was it important to them? How was it going to be helpful to them in their learning?

After only a few children had spoken, we made them stop so that we could find clipboards and pens. Their responses were impressive; we needed to write them down. We were immediately struck by the thoughtfulness they had shown in choosing goals and their awareness of why the goals would be helpful to them in real ways.

Here are some of their sharings:

LUCY: I will write smaller. I've never done it before. I have more space to write what I say.

FRED: I will write the way I talk. This way sounds more interesting.

GEORGIANNA: I will write a make-believe story. I wanted to try it again.

CHARLES: I will write a make-believe story. I've never done it before.

JIMMY: I will read a nonfiction book. I never read a nonfiction book before.

ALICE: I will not sit by Maria or Lisa at Communications Time. When I do sit by Lisa and Maria, sometimes I talk and I don't get much done.

PATRICK: When I read, I will fix my mouth to say the beginnings of words. It helps me to figure out the words I don't know.

ROBBIE: I will write a poem book. I wanted to make another book and I hadn't ever done a poem book.

TOM: I will write more each day and I wanted it because I like to write in my day book. So, I wanted to write a lot.

SUSIE: I will finish my *One Mouse* story and edit it and publish it. When I write down words in my dictionary, next time when I want to use that word, I know how to spell it.

MARK: I will write three interesting sentences each day. Last year I was the first one done. I wanted this goal so I would have more to think about. I will have to think of three things.

JOANNA: I will do a poster on black history. I've been reading a lot about black history and I thought I'd do a poster and advertise it. At my Goal Conference, I decided to read more and do a poster.

TIM: I will use action in my story, so that people will say they feel like they are at the scene.

HEATHER: I will sit alone at Communications Workshop. Every time I sit with my friends they talk to me and I fool around, so I have to start over each day.

JACK: I will write at least one page in my day book every day. Next year I'll be having to write more than one page. So, I'm getting ready.

DOUG: I will read a nonfiction book and make a poster of it. I haven't done that goal before. I really like making posters. I made one at home about a farm.

JAN: I will sit alone at Communications. If I sit by somebody they need help. If I help them I don't get my work done.

MARIA: I will read a nonfiction book and make a poster of it. I usually never get to do something like that.

LISA: I will try to write another poem. I haven't written many.

We often encourage the children to be thinking about their goals. We remind them at the beginning of work times to check their goals so that they will be sure to work on them. We also use periodic informal reminders, such as asking after Quiet Reading Time, "Did anyone work on a reading goal today? Would you tell us about it?" When a child shows us his writing after writing time we might say, "Tell me how you have worked on one of your writing goals in this piece of writing today."

Setting goals helps children think about their learning. With choice comes responsibility. Children become engaged in their learning. They see their working times as opportunities to help themselves become better readers and writers, and as Susan told her mother, they are upset when their Communications Workshop time is shortened.

Charles gives another very important reason for having goal-setting conferences: "When I get to have choices in what I do, I am happy!"

Daily Reflections and Homework

In addition to setting their own literacy goals, the children are asked every day to look at the work they are doing and to question how they are helping themselves grow as learners. From Talking Journal Time to the End of the Day Question, they are frequently asked to consider what they are doing and why they are doing it. They are asked to think about their progress as learners and to plan what they need to do next. They are expected to see themselves as the ones in charge of their learning and to take responsibility for the choices they make. They evaluate their projects, write about their mathematical thinking, question how they can make their writing better, and challenge themselves in their reading.

One day Ellen showed us how she had been reflecting on her learning. She shared her day book with Penny, showing how she had used our mini-lesson of the day before to help her improve her writing. Penny and I had decided to do this particular mini-lesson because we had noticed that the children had been writing a lot about the happenings in their personal lives in their day books. We felt that perhaps with some encouragement they would add those details that would help to make their stories more interesting to their audience. In the mini-lesson Penny and I had had a conversation about how Penny could make her story of a normal occurrence at her house—in this case, phone calls to her daughters—interesting to the reader. Penny told a little about what she wanted to say, and I suggested that Penny might reveal her feelings in her story. It's always interesting when the writer shows us what she is feeling. The children had other ideas for what she could do: put conversation in her story, use interesting words, and use good descriptions so the readers could get a picture of what she was telling them. We ended our discussion with a summary of those suggestions, and we began the writing portion of our Communications Workshop.

The next day, at the end of Communications Workshop, Ellen came to Penny with her story (Figure 7–4). "Look what I did today!" she proudly exclaimed. "I used everything we talked about yesterday that would help make a story interesting. I think it's the most interesting story I ever wrote."

Penny read Ellen's story about a present she had received. Ellen had used all four ideas in her writing. There was conversation. There were interesting words (*shocked, gasp*). There were enough details to give Penny a glimpse of the scene Ellen was describing, and her writing left no doubt as to the feelings she and her mother were experiencing.

Penny returned Ellen's day book. "I like the way you worked on your writing today. You really made an effort to use all that you heard in the mini-lesson. This story is very interesting. I enjoyed reading it, especially the part where your mother gasps. She sounds as shocked as you were! I also like the way you used conversation."

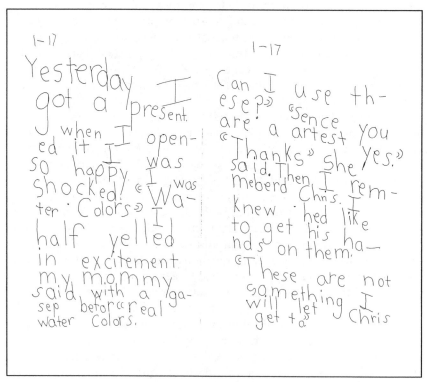

Figure 7–4

"Thanks. Is it okay if I take my day book home tonight to show this story to my mom?" Ellen asked.

"Sure you can," agreed Penny. "Your mom will be proud that you are thinking so hard about how to make your writing better. But be sure to bring your day book back tomorrow. Maybe you could share this story for our mini-lesson."

"All right!" exclaimed Ellen as she went to put her day book into her backpack for the trip home.

One other very significant way that the children demonstrate their ability to take charge of their learning is by doing their homework: a one-page message that is a reproduction of the Morning Message we worked on that day. The children are asked to read the message to their parents and to fill in the five words left blank. Sometimes they are also asked to use the back of the paper to write or draw an answer to a question on the front. Many children will demonstrate what they know about the phonics, writing conventions, and their reading on their homework. They show this knowledge by circling the words they can read, separating compound words into their two parts, noting beginning blends or digraphs, underlining all the nouns on the page, and in many other ways. What the children notice on their homework shows us how seriously they take their commitment to be in charge of their own learning. Their noticings change as they challenge themselves to grow as readers and writers. Our emergent readers will focus on circling the letters that are in their names or other letters they know. They might find instances where a word is repeated on the homework. Independent readers may notice the punctuation we have used and explain why a question mark, comma, or exclamation mark was used. Children who are working on their spelling may note that they spelled a word from the homework "with their eyes closed" for their parents. The noticings are as varied as the children's needs.

In his homework, Carter shows us that he knows *child* is the root word in *children* and that *boxcar* is a compound word (Figure 7–5). He makes us aware of his knowledge of words by underlining the little words that he has found in larger ones. It was his choice to add these noticings to his homework. He had taken the responsibility to share with us his understanding of the words.

The children's answers to the homework questions also show us how they perceive their literacy growth and how they are working toward becoming even better communicators. Our younger children most often use pictures to share their ideas with us. Invented spelling next becomes the norm as the children progress toward standard spelling. The children also demonstrate to us through their answers how they are growing as thinkers and problem solvers. These homework answers

Name Carter   January 24

Dear (Children,)

    Usually, the a~~thor~~ of a book has a message or lesson to tell. The message in a story is called its (theme.)

The Boxcar Children has

two themes.. They are

independence and co-operation.

What do you think Gertrude Chandler Warner wanted us to learn about independence and co-operation?   Love,
                        Jane and Penny

Figure 7–5

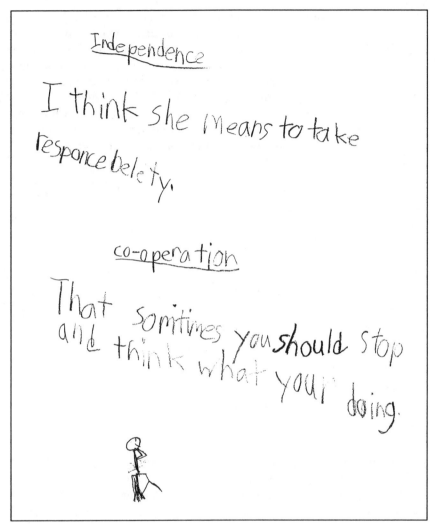

Figure 7–6

are also an indicator of how seriously they take their commitment to be in charge of their own learning. In Figure 7–6, Carter shows what he has done to take ownership of his learning.

Portfolios

Around the time that we began Goal Conferences with the children, we also decided that it was time to institute portfolios as another way to value the children's learning. Portfolios were all the rage, and we felt just a little guilty that we had not yet incorporated them into our program.

We began with a week of sharing what we value. The children were amazing in their enthusiasm for this project. Their suggestions soon filled a large piece of orange paper that was taped to the board. Penny and I showed the children our portfolios and asked if they would like to create portfolios of their work. We worked in small groups to list possibilities for a literacy portfolio. When we came together as a large group we found that each group had expressed similar ideas, and we collected a long list of possibilities. It included:

- Photocopies of favorite stories we have written about important things
- Titles of favorite books we can read or listen to
- Math papers
- Reading tests
- Communications Workshop Goals
- Tapes of us reading
- Illustrations
- Blue spelling cards
- Book reviews from our literature logs
- Poems we have written
- Personal information and photographs
- Favorite books

Penny and I cleaned out my two-drawer filing cabinet and bought each child a hanging file folder to use as a portfolio. We were ready for business. The children were shown where the files were located and told that they had free access to them. They could put in material whenever they wanted, and they could look over what was there whenever they wanted.

The first couple of months the children often went to the file cabinet to add to their portfolios or to check out what was there. It seemed that every piece of work they were doing that was not in a log or day book ended up in the children's portfolios.

Then the children began to ask if they could take their work home. They missed sharing their work with their parents on the day they did it. They missed seeing their work decorating their refrigerators at home. The portfolios stopped getting fatter. At the end of the year the children cleaned them out and took all their treasured work home.

The next year the children were less anxious to fill up their portfolios. They preferred taking their work home as it was completed. The portfolios became merely a place to store the Goal Conference Sheets, their editing and publishing forms, and the audiotapes they used to tape their reading. Most of the children felt no need for keeping other work in a portfolio at school. They had a greater need to take the fruits of their labors home.

Penny and I decided that this was okay. The portfolios were the children's. They could determine what went in them. We did decide that we would institute two forms to record some of their reading and writing each year. We use these forms twice a year now.

My Writing

Author: _____ Date: _____

Title: _____

This is why I chose this piece:

The things I like about my writing are:

This is how I could improve it.

Books I Read

Reader: _____ Date: _____

My favorite books to read on my own this quarter were:

1. _____

2. _____

I enjoyed them because:

1. _____

_____

_____

2. _____

_____

_____

We are happy with our scaled-down portfolios. The children have shown us that it is not necessary to have fat portfolios to show that they are growing as learners. They show us their growth every day. All we need to remember to do is to look and see what is happening in our classrooms.

Fortunately, we have many visitors who remind us of just what it is we need to be looking at. Shirley is a student at the University of Arizona. She was staying in the central Maine area for a few weeks in January and asked if she could visit our class for a few days. The few days turned into two wonderful weeks, with Shirley becoming a valued member of our multiage family. Her presence in our room was good both for us and for the children. She has the gift of knowing the "teachable moment" and of interacting in a positive manner with the children.

Her last day with us came all too soon, but we understood that she needed to return to her studies in Arizona. After school that day, Penny and I tried to tell her how special her visit had been for us, but she made it even more special by leaving us with something to think about. Her parting words: "What I like most about your program is that the kids want to learn."

Penny and I considered this. We thought over the children's behaviors during the time Shirley was here. We could remember several instances when it seemed to us that the children were ready to do anything but learn. After all, during the time Shirley was here we had experienced below-zero temperatures, which meant no recess for over a week. There had been two snowstorms, but no snow days off, and it was also the period of the full moon. The children were very itchy—and understandably so!

We continued to reflect on the children's work in light of Shirley's comment. We discussed what Shirley had seen during her two weeks with us. It had taken a few extra minutes for the children to settle down at Morning Meetings, but for the most part the children had been their usual selves at Morning Message, thoughtful about its content, anxious to share what they knew and to spell the missing words. Choice Time had seemed noisy, but when we looked around everyone seemed to be working happily and cooperatively. At Investigation Time the children had been actively engaged in their work, even though some of that activity was not always productive. Math Time had been filled with some fidgety children (their bodies knew they had not had recess!). Yet they had also been eager workers and thinkers. And during Communications Workshops the children had worked on their literacy goals and could tell us what they were doing and why. It may have taken a little longer than usual for them to get down to their work, but they had been reading and writing up to their usual standards.

Shirley had seen the involvement of the children in their work. She had been watching their commitment to learning, while we were focused on their itchy behavior. She reminded us of what is truly important. She made us remember that when the children are given ownership of their work, they will take the responsibility of doing it well. They are autonomous learners, making their choices because those choices are right for them, not because a teacher has told them what choice to make.

Looking at the Learner 8

Penelle Chase

Recently Jane and I were invited to speak about our multiage classroom at the annual conference of the Maine School Management Association. Though we were used to "talking multiage" to teachers, we were particularly enthused about sharing our ideas about multiage education with this audience of school board members, principals, and superintendents. We constructed our talk around the central elements of our multiage program, focusing on a catchy theme of three C's: *Community, Curriculum,* and *Continuity.* These were the elements that had emerged as strong benefits for us in the early stages of working in multiage settings. As it turned out, we found ourselves elaborating even more thoroughly on a fourth *C,* the concept of student *Choice,* a major ingredient in our teaching that has been developing over the years. We supported our comments about student ownership with numerous slides of our students involved in their learning as they worked independently and chose activities during the school day.

In spite of a short-lived projector foul-up midway through our talk, the presentation went well. Judging from the questions and comments from members of the audience, we were confident that we had presented a convincing argument for student participation in the learning process. Our usual public-speaking jitters began to subside as we packed up our materials and prepared to leave.

Then a whirlwind hit. I cringed as I sighted an older woman determinedly advancing upon our table. "What do you do about the kindergartners?" she shrilled at me. "I mean, what are you doing to teach them to read? You can't just give them choices all day long and expect them to learn to read. You've got to *teach* these little ones. I know, because I've been a teaching principal in a primary school for twenty-four years."

I quailed and looked to Jane for support. Unfortunately, Jane was busy with a calm-appearing individual at the other end of the table. I opened my mouth, and the woman began again. "When do you teach them their letters and their sounds? How do you keep track of the words they know? How do you know where they *are*?"

Hopeless in confrontational situations, I felt my mind go blank. "We don't keep track," I finally squeaked out. Then, gaining a little momentum, I went on in a rush. "We don't have to keep track to know they are learning. We watch them, we listen to them. We hear them reading, we see them writing. We notice the things children are learning every day. We don't have to keep track of anything!"

"Hmmph! That's not teaching!" she announced. And she turned and left as quickly as she had come.

"What was that all about?" Jane was finally at my side.

"Oh, you know," I groaned. "Just another one who wants to know how we know that the children are learning. She said that we weren't teaching if we didn't keep track!"

"Well, what did you tell her?"

"She didn't wait for me to tell her much! She left in a huff before I could get my head together."

"Well, don't worry about it," Jane advised. "The children *are* learning. That's what's important."

I didn't worry, but I did continue to ponder the dilemma. The "How do you know your students are learning?" question was one that surfaced in one form or another fairly often. We heard it from teachers who visited our program: "What do you do for record keeping? Do you have skills checklists?" We heard it from prospective parents: "How do the kids do after they leave your program?" We heard it from administrators: "Do your students score favorably on standardized tests?" We heard it from our working colleagues: "How do you know if a child needs to be retained or needs resource room help?"

Dealing with questions like these has been a tricky balancing act between trusting that our students are learning and proving it to the world. We know that our students can be in charge of their learning and of constructing knowledge. We are convinced that such ownership is the only way people become self-sufficient learners. Encouraging our students to value their own learning is far more important to us than our assessing of that learning. We have no compulsion to measure our students' learning against the artificial yardsticks of standardized testing, skills inventories, or diagnostic surveys. We find no need to compare one student with another. We do not expect our students to be synchronized to all learn the same things at the same time.

We feel comfortable looking at children as entities unto themselves, whose accomplishments speak for themselves. Their writing in day books, their reflections in investigations and literature logs, their contributions to discussions, their verbalized thought processes, their interactions with others, their Goals Conferences, their shared ideas, along with their drawings, paintings, constructions, songs, smiles, and tears speak to us. The children themselves are living, breathing portfolios. They and what they do every day and over time are the records of their learning.

The hang-up for the world at large is that this knowledge of the learner is not easy to access. Children are far too bulky (and balky) to be conveniently filed in file folders. Even their work is often too voluminous and cumbersome to store. Besides, most of the children's creations are so valuable to them that they are taken home to be shared with families. The children consent to storing some things in their portfolios, they tape themselves reading, they maintain goal sheets and math folders. Jane and I make copies of a few work samples and diligently file them away. More often, however, we find ourselves noting our observations and impressions of children in our writing and in our talking. This informal system works for us as teachers. It works, as well, for the parents of our children, who see firsthand and hear from us what their children are learning, and who feel comfortable in speaking frankly with us if they have concerns about the process. And, most important of all, it works for the students themselves. Because they take responsibility for their learning, they are aware of that learning. They learn because they want to learn.

Perhaps our system is too simple to be believable. Educators are accustomed to elaborate record-keeping stratagems. It seems that the more paper that is produced, the more concrete evidence exists that someone is learning something, or at least that someone is trying to teach something. Over the years we found that we do not need this paper. Our school district requires that we administer an analytical reading inventory, that we assess math objectives with a host of district-created tests, that we subject our oldest students to standardized achievement testing. Jane jokes bleakly that she could save our school district a lot of money; she could predict the results of these tests without the district wasting the money to buy them. And it is true. For us, the proof is in the pudding. You really cannot appreciate it until you taste it. Let me try to give you a "taste" of two of our students, Rebecca and Bryant, whose paths through our classrooms have been strikingly different. They have learned in their unique ways as they have grown in our program over the years. We only wish that you could meet them in real life, to know them as people and to see them as learners.

Rebecca

Rebecca couldn't wait to come to school as a full-fledged member of our class. Her brother, Adam, was already with us, so Rebecca knew what to expect. She had been to the farm to plant and weed pumpkins, she had played happily in the classrooms when her parents came for conferences or to pick up Adam after school. She knew what the class was doing, because school was important to Adam and he talked about it at home. Now Rebecca was five years old and would be a first-year student in my room while her brother, Adam, would be a third-year student in Jane's.

On an August evening a few days before school was to begin, Rebecca came with her family to the Open House in our classroom. She was dressed up in long ruffled skirt, braids, and red cowgirl boots. In a matter of minutes as I greeted Rebecca's parents and Adam wandered over to Jane's room, Rebecca rounded up paper and crayons and sat down at a table to get to work. She has been busy ever since.

Rebecca is now a third-year student. She is a child with many gifts. She is an artist, a writer, a storyteller, a poet, a thinker, a reader, an observer, a mathematician, a dancer, a dreamer. Watching her develop these gifts during her time with us has been a wonderful experience. During the October conference of her first year with us I shared these Conference Notes with Rebecca's parents:

> Rebecca waltzes in here every day, self-confident and knowing exactly what she's about. She is happy all morning, both at playing and work-ing times. She chooses a variety of activities to do at Choice Time—blocks, dollhouse, etc.—but she leans toward the arts, painting, draw-ing, and creating with her hands. She certainly is gifted in these areas.
>
> Rebecca is eager to share stories at Talking Journal Time—her turn never seems quite long enough for her to tell everything she would like to tell. She is always thinking and is eager to participate in discussions. Rebecca is paying close attention at message time; it is obvious that she is absorbing a great deal of literacy learning. We think that she is off to a great start in school, and we are enjoying her very much!

It was fun telling Rebecca's parents about Rebecca's fir months of school. It was so obvious that she was having the time of her life. Rebec-ca's parents agreed that Rebecca was enthusiastic about school. We talked about their aspirations for Rebecca. As we had requested, they had set down their year's goals for her: that she recognize letters and sounds, that she appreciate learning activities, that she improve her speech (*r* and *l* sounds especially), and that she participate in an art class. They knew that Rebecca was eager to start staying at school for a full day, because the art "special class" happened in the afternoon. She was also eager to do more reading and writing during our Communications Workshop in the afternoon. We agreed that Rebecca would definitely be ready for staying all day when the time came. The first "all day" would be at the end of January. Then we would add on an extra "all day" every few weeks as we progressed into spring.

Our predictions were borne out as Rebecca began staying at school for full days. Rebecca was a real "school" person, both easy and exciting to have around. She liked everything about school: the work, the play, the socializing, the thinking. Her creative ideas contributed to the aura in the classroom as an environment for learning. In March I wrote these comments at parent conference time:

> Rebecca continues to be an eager and enthusiastic learner. She is attentive and thoughtful during discussions and at message time. She is anxious to participate and expresses herself well; her comments often promote further discussion among the other students.
>
> Rebecca enjoys the activities we do here. She socializes happily during Choice Time, at recess, and at working times. She puts a lot of energy into her work and is proud of the results. She reveled in the art theme we have just completed! But she seems to be equally enthused about *Charlotte's Web*. We are happy that she is sound-spelling with confidence on her homework and in her day book; she chooses writing and drawing activities often during Choice Time.
>
> In math, Rebecca's group has worked on counting, free exploring number tubs, patterning, and graphs. She is actively involved at math time and demonstrates a good understanding of concepts.
>
> We are happy to have such a good-natured, deep-thinking risk taker in our midst!

Rebecca's mother responded with these comments:

> Rebecca simply loves school. She comes home happy every day and full of enthusiasm about her work and her friends. We are so proud of her accomplishments in her work with letters and sound spelling. Sometimes she just amazes us with what she can do! Thank you!

And Rebecca dictated this:

> I love everything about school. I mostly like the art and when we studied about the body.

Rebecca's early writings and drawings in her day book illustrate her facility with literacy. When the first-year students received their first day books, Rebecca listened attentively as a third-year student, Serene, helped with the mini-lesson explaining how to use them. "You have to write about something important to you," Serene instructed. Rebecca took these words to heart. Her first six entries focused on the important people and animals in her life. "I have daddy How [who] IS onpooea [important]" (1/21). "I have mom How IS onpooea" (2/4). She continued in this vein until she had recognized each human and animal family member. By early June she showed that she was comfortably soundspelling as she continued to write about what was important to her: "I aef [have] tow [two] ous [loose] tef [teeth] aet [at] my top if [of] my meof [mouth]" (6/2). She named these two teeth Rebecca and Erin (after her best friend), and in due time, thankfully, they fell out.

Rebecca wanted to be a reader and writer. She realized that paying attention to the Morning Message lesson would help her accomplish these goals, so she attended rigorously as we read the message together, spelled the words, discussed letter sounds, and noticed structural elements of the language. She was innately interested in the content of the message, too, from the point of view of the information it imparted, as well as its stylistic features. On the last day of school in her yearbook Rebecca responds to the prompt *The best thing I did was when I . . .* with these words: "Lisesan to Jane and Penny because I lod [learned] a lot"— beautifully illustrated with a picture of children sitting on the rug attending to the Morning Message. Rebecca had an ear for language. She loved the choral work we did with poems and songs during meeting time. She enjoyed hearing stories, often bringing books from home to share with the class. Being outgoing by nature, she participated eagerly at Investigations Workshop and in Literature Group activities. She expressed her opinions, she asked questions, she took risks as she began to do her own spelling on homework papers. Rebecca's first year progressed in a happy-go-lucky fashion, with Rebecca virtually soaking up concepts, skills, and ideas around her.

Rebecca embraced school with open arms again as her second year began. She was anxious to get back to her best friend, Erin, whom she wrote about in her day book on the first day of school. In our class the only direction for topic selection in day books is "to write about something important to you." Choosing a topic was never difficult for Rebecca, because she was interested in so many things. She wrote about her family: "I haved a weard jowem [dream] abaout ADAM" (9/22). She wrote about people and things she liked: "I like the red wiet and blue Fag" (10/11). "I like Penny and. Penny like me to. I like Penny because Penny is nisc to me and Penny likes me" (10/12). She used interesting words and included emotions in her writing: "mom ws Fitind [frightened] I ws going to go dan the fory [falls]!" (10/13). She wrote autobiographical entries: "Today my mom and Dad tok me to School for a foing [thing] yf Penny" (10/20). Her stories began to get longer: "I have a dllwe [dolly]. I haved it for a Lorllg time. I haved it seach I ws a baby. my parerets gaf it to me. my mom mad me a sorckt [skirt]. A corderyro [corduroy] sorckt"(10/21).

Rebecca had her first goal-setting conference with me at the end of September. At that time she chose to practice one of the Wright Group books, *My Sloppy Tiger*, for a reading goal. She decided that in writing she would "write some more stories" and "put spaces between my words." On October 13, we had a goal review conference. Rebecca had worked on *My Sloppy Tiger* at Quiet Reading and Read with a Friend times during Communications Workshop. She read some of it aloud to me, and I saw that she was using reading strategies well. Still, the book was a little challenging for her, and she preferred reading some of the other Wright Group books she had been practicing. She decided to practice *Smarty Pants* during the next goal period. Her writing goal would be: "I will think of new things to write about."

During the October conference with Rebecca's parents, I shared my thoughts on Rebecca's literacy learning:

> Rebecca's good listening at message time has helped her in her reading and writing. She is enthusiastic about learning to read. She chooses a variety of books to practice during Communications Workshop, and she really works at them. She enjoys reading aloud with friends, as well. She has picked out a few books to concentrate on for goals. I see her using excellent reading strategies: context, picture clues, sounding out. She is equally involved in writing. Her present goal is to "think of new things to write about." She wants to try more make-believe stories. Rebecca is working hard on sound spelling and she is beginning to spell some sight words conventionally.

We talked, too, about Rebecca's high level of involvement in everything we did at school, from our theme work to her personal goals and projects. Rebecca's parents were worried about Rebecca's speech. Though she had some articulation difficulties, it was easy to understand her and she was not self-conscious about talking. However, they were concerned that her speech would interfere with her learning to spell and read. We decided that it would be best to have her screened again by the speech therapist.

In late October when we were studying dinosaurs, Rebecca embarked on a nonfiction dinosaur story. Her knowledge simply poured out, and she covered page after page with words and pictures. In three days she had completed nineteen pages. To conclude her story Rebecca shared her views on the demise of the dinosaur: "The Dinosaurs are not aiof [alive] naiy [now]. They are dad. I'm gad they will not kam bek. Bat Peow [people] fail [find] bobasns [bones]. And some bobasns are in the meyseans [museums]. You cen see forosns [fossils] aoef Dinosaurs. They are net to. Ef Dinosaur aer sill alif we wad not be alif. I know thes is theoeu [true]." Rebecca was proud of this effort and decided that it would be her first piece to edit and publish. At our third Goals Conference she specified "I will edit and publish my dinosaur story" as a writing goal along with "I will put periods where they belong."

Learning to read and write were happening naturally for Rebecca in this rich environment. She seized opportunities to pursue literacy activities. I commented in my day book on Rebecca's initiative and her devotion to learning.

Penny's Day Book 11/13

Rebecca does lots of reading, writing, and drawing for Choice Time. She conceived the idea of making a book about school, and asked if we could have it up for a choice. *Rebecca's Book* went up on the board as a choice, and each day Rebecca worked with the person who signed up. The choice was up for about a week—Erin and Sandra signed up and did pages. The book was about all the things the girls liked about school. It was interesting to note how Rebecca's spelling improved as the book progressed. She misspelled *school* for several pages, then all of a sudden she was spelling it conventionally. I asked her why she had begun spelling it differently, and she said she had seen how Sandra was spelling the word.

Rebecca is enthused about the dinosaur theme and school in general. She wrote recently in her day book: "Now we are sadeing Dinosaurs And I am glad. And Penny and Jane are glad we are laneing a lot of things of them. Penny and Jane hlpe us on Goals and the ather choices. Penny and Jane like are shool I do think they do."

Rebecca stuck close by Erin at Choice Time for the first six weeks of school. Then I noticed that she was signing up for some different choices. However, they are still often together. Sometimes they play with blocks or Legos. They love the dinosaur museum. Erin and Rebecca made the dinosaur sounds tape to go in the Little Room museum. They also picked out books to go in there for research. They chose to work together on their dinosaur research project, too. They made what they called a "display," cutting off the top and front of a large cardboard box and creating a dinosaur environment with construction paper and clay. They placed many plastic dinosaur figures in this setting. In their presentation they told what they knew about some of the dinosaurs. When we asked the girls to evaluate their project, Rebecca said, "If we could not crowd it up too much, it would be better. We could have talked about more things." And Erin agreed, "Yeah, we could have told more details about each dinosaur."

These girls have a very caring relationship. When Erin was in with her mother at conference time, it came out that Erin was a little worried about Rebecca. Erin said that Rebecca was sad about her reading ability. Evidently, Rebecca felt that she should be reading better than she was. I wondered if perhaps Rebecca was comparing herself to Erin, who is a very accomplished reader for her age. I assured Erin that Rebecca was reading very well, and we both planned to give more emotional support to Rebecca. I was glad to have this new insight into another facet of the seemingly happy-go-lucky Rebecca.

The winter of Rebecca's second year was a breakthrough period for her. Her dinosaur story editing experience encouraged her to take more control of her writing. By early December she began writing a make-believe space story, "Space Girl and Comet Boy." She chose more sophisticated goals to work on: "I will put more details in my space story" and "I will look up some common words in my dictionary." For weeks she continued to work on this story and its sequel, "Space Girl and Comet Boy II," experimenting with action, dialogue, and plot. She began to spell more words conventionally, to use capital letters more appropriately, and to utilize a variety of punctuation marks. Rebecca was now reading the Wright Group books with ease. She decided that she would branch out and try to read some other fiction picture books and poetry books.

The speech therapist evaluated Rebecca's articulation and expression. She found Rebecca's expressive vocabulary to be very advanced, and she thought she would probably outgrow her articulation problems. Together we looked at Rebecca's writing, and our analysis was that Rebecca's speech problems were not interfering seriously with her spelling. Though her sound-spelled words reflected some of her articulation differences, her spelling was becoming more conventional all the time. Rebecca's parents were reassured by this news.

At the turn of the year we were immersed in our family histories theme. Typically, Rebecca's involvement in our theme work spilled over into other parts of our day. She spent several Choice Time periods happily working on a book about all the people in her family. The day she worked on the section about her mom, she told me: "I might have to do three pages this time. I am putting in lots of details. I know a lot about that mom of mine." Her happy, productive times were punctuated by occasional "low" periods, when nothing seemed right with her world. Perhaps it was winter blahs or maybe growing pains. We tried to help her pinpoint a particular problem, without much success. "I am brother sick!" was her only voiced lament. Adam was now in the intermediate multiage class. Catching a glimpse of him across our crowded cafeteria every day at lunch would often set Rebecca off. All our talk could not assuage her "brother-sickness." When we assured her that she would soon be seeing her brother after school, she was still not soothed. "He doesn't do the stuff I do," she maintained. "He only wants to do his Cub Scout stuff. I have to just play with Philip." Being at this awkward stage of in-betweenness—too young for the older brother and too mature for the younger one—was devastating to Rebecca, who loved her siblings so much. On some days her world seemed to be falling apart.

Then Rebecca learned to read, and suddenly she had other things to think about. Of course, Rebecca had been reading for months, but in January she learned to read the way *she* wanted to read. I wrote about the event in my day book.

Penny's Day Book—January 23

Rebecca wanted me to sit next to her at Communications time today. I told her to save me a place. At Quiet Reading time she was reading *Mouse Soup*. She asked me to tell her several words, and she wanted to read with me at Read with a Friend Time. She read *Mouse Soup* aloud to me very fluently. She told me that this was one of her favorite books. "I had this book in my pile, so I could look at the pictures. But when you said to us to be sure to have some books to practice for your goals, I decided I will not just look at the pictures, I will try to read the words. I said, 'Penny read this book to us, so I guess I'll give it a try!' I did, and I read one word and one word and one word . . . I can read it, and it's a chapter book, too!"

Mouse Soup was in Rebecca's hands constantly during the next week. She read it every chance she could get: before school, at Communications, while waiting for her bus to be called, going out the door, on the bus. After that week, she knew she had mastered that book, and she began to choose other challenging books to work on for goal books.

As spring came on, we noticed that Rebecca was no longer having her "sad days." Perhaps she had come to terms with her relationship with Adam. He was still in her thoughts, however. One Choice Time she worked on a book for him. It was written, illustrated, and stapled together all in one day, ready to be taken home to Adam.

ADAm's fish. By Rebecca
ADAm's fish. Dedicated to ADAM by Rebecca
ADAm got a fish tack [tank].
We got Him a fish to go in it.
He put it in the tack.
It will swimm up to Him.
One day it was diing. ADAm kid [cried].
It died. ADam was sad.

The first-year students were coming all day most days now, and Rebecca enjoyed her role of being one of the responsible "older kids." She eagerly assisted anyone who needed help, and she set an excellent example as an involved learner.

Rebecca and I met at the end of May for a goal review conference. We talked together about her current goals, we looked at her day book, and

I listened to her read. When we realized that this was to be the last goal-setting conference of the school year, Rebecca suggested that she write her own goals. So I proceeded with my conference with Shelby, as Rebecca sat beside me filling out her goals sheet. I noticed her flipping through the sheaf of previous goal-setting forms to check on spellings of words. When I turned back to Rebecca she was finished and showed me what she produced (see Figure 8–1).

I was impressed with the goals that Rebecca had figured out on her own. I thought that she had chosen appropriately challenging books to practice. I was pleased that she had decided to tape-record her reading; I thought that she would probably be impressed when she listened to herself. I was glad that she planned to use her dictionary more frequently, and I was impressed that she realized she could locate conventional spellings of words in books she had read. I noticed that Rebecca was beginning to care more about what her writing looked like. In her second writing goal she had decided that she was ready to write on lines; she would use a ruler to rule her day book pages as she wrote. I was

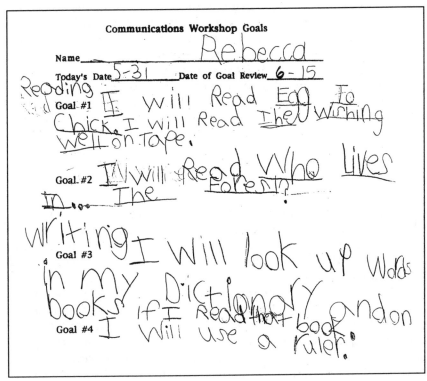

Figure 8–1

gratified to see Rebecca's awareness of her literacy needs, along with her plans to strengthen her learning.

Rebecca's self-reflection did not surprise me. She is a perceptive child who thinks deeply about issues affecting her and other people. In class discussions Rebecca almost always has a thoughtful contribution. She thinks about what others say, she thinks about what she reads, and she thinks about the work we do in class. Her memory is prodigious, and she often connects past knowledge to her activities of the moment. In that second year with us we were frequently amazed by Rebecca's ability to "put it all together." One day Rebecca spent an entire Choice Time constructing a sturdy wall with blocks. "Now that took a lot of hard work!" she announced as she completed it. "I feel like a real dog working like that!" This comment showed us that Rebecca had internalized the phrase *dog-tired*, which we had discussed in a mini-lesson the day before. Rebecca's whimsical use of language and her sense of humor are highlights of her personality.

Rebecca's second year with us drew to a close. She was a happy, self-confident student who would be excited to rejoin us the following fall. We looked forward to having her return as one of the oldest students, who would be a good role model for the younger children as she continued to make strides in her own learning. We liked having Rebecca around. Her sensitive, caring nature was obvious in her dealings with both her home family and her school family.

Rebecca was flourishing in an environment where she was free to express herself in all areas of her development. Without any formal "keeping track," the results of this child's engagement in her learning were obvious.

Bryant

Bryant, too, knew all about the multiage class before he entered school. His brother, Stephen, had been in our class, and Bryant had often accompanied his mother when she came in to help out in our classrooms. His well-worn friend, Teddy Bear, usually came, too. Bryant joined in with whatever Literature Group his mom was leading. He listened raptly to the story and seriously offered his perspectives during the discussion that followed. Bryant enjoyed talking, and people of all ages enjoyed listening to him. If he got bored during lit group, he sometimes went looking for better entertainment. As often as not, after school Bryant's mom would find him in the office, regaling the secretaries and principals with stories. Later, she would bring Bryant back to the classroom to retrieve Teddy Bear, forgotten in a corner.

"Isn't he verbal!" people would often remark in the first days of Bryant's official schooling. "The things he comes out with!" Bryant's tininess was remarkable, too. No one could believe that such words of wisdom could come from one so small. What he lacked in stature he made up for in self-concept. Bryant aspired to be a professional basketball player, and Michael Jordan was his idol. Bryant demonstrated his basketball "moves" with aplomb occasionally throughout the day; he was very coordinated. Bryant's fine motor skills were less developed. He found holding a pencil and writing to be a frustrating exercise. He avoided writing whenever he could, even adopting "B.R." rather than "Bryant" as his signature for signing up for Choice Time, for labeling his cubby, and for identifying his homework papers. He did not seem at all interested in trying to write, and his drawings were sketchy and quick as well.

In the beginning, though, Bryant did not find school too hard to take. Coming for half a day was just right for him. The morning consisted of Talking Journal, Morning Meeting, Choice Time, Investigations Workshop, and recess. The sitting-down time of Morning Meeting got a tad long for him, but he found that he still had plenty of time to converse and play at other times during the morning. We did not pressure Bryant to write, either at school or at home. He did drawings in his investigations log, and he usually dictated the words to fill in the blanks on his homework paper. His brother, Stephen, or Mom or Dad did the actual writing. In the goals for the year that Bryant's parents had written, they had hoped that Bryant would "Gain good pencil control." Fortunately, they had also hoped that he would "Be comfortable and happy with the classroom setting" and "Build on his social skills." I was confident and relieved that they saw these last two goals as being more important than demanding that Bryant write before he was ready.

For the first fall conference I wrote these notes:

> Since he has been a frequent visitor in the past, Bryant has had an extra easy time starting school in our multiage class. He is happy and mellow during both playing and working times. Building with blocks and the big bricks are his favorite Choice Time activities. Recess time is great for him, too. Bryant is happiest when his sidekick, Ronnie, is close at hand, but he plays and works with other children as well.
>
> Bryant is interested in everything we do. He listens well at message time, and he "notices" a lot in the written text of the message. He actively participates in group theme work, and he has ideas to share in most discussions. He is a great storyteller—he would like to have more time to talk at Talking Journal Time!
>
> Bryant's fine motor skills are improving. He is taking more time with his pictures. Occasionally, he tries to write a little, but writing is clearly not his favorite thing!

As winter came on Jane and I were a little hesitant at the thought of Bryant staying at school for the full day. We had observed that his energy seemed to flag late in the morning, and we sensed that he needed more free play time than our afternoon sessions would offer him. In January we talked it over with Bryant's parents. They shared our hesitancy, but they were living with a boy who *wanted* to come to school all day. Bryant was sure! We decided to give it a try, knowing that if it didn't work out, Bryant could resume the half-day schedule.

So, beginning in January, and during the ensuing winter and early spring, Bryant was staying at school all day two days a week. Initially, he was very content. He enjoyed the hands-on math activities that Jane's group did, and he showed a good grasp of math concepts. At reading time during the afternoon Communications Workshop he listened intently at story time, he browsed happily through a large variety of books at Quiet Reading Time, and he and his pal, Ronnie, paired up to look at books together at Reading with a Friend Time. At writing time Bryant made elaborate pictures in his day book, and he wrote elaborate stories to accompany them. His writing was typical of a beginning writer, usually strings of capital letters, sometimes with a few words interspersed in the text. In early February at sharing time he "read" a long story about going to a basketball game with his family. This was the text: "MiAEELN MiiEEF NO YES WILL OMM MOM MC" (2/4).

Bryant's writing continued in this vein throughout the spring, with true stories about his family, fantastic basketball stories, and detailed accounts of villains who met their match. By mid-April his stories were taking just as long to tell at sharing time, but the writing was dwindling. Sometimes he worked hard at constructing a few "fancy" letters in block style or incorporating pictures into the letter formation. He was not yet attempting to sound-spell, he did not consult his dictionary for help with words, and only rarely did he ask for a word to be written in his dictionary. This Ninja Turtle story is typical of his writing at that time: "MCE-MEFIG" (4/22). Bryant sometimes acted dispirited in the afternoon; we wondered if his early enthusiasm for the all-day experience was beginning to wane a bit. At conference time at the end of April, I shared these observations with Bryant's parents:

> Bryant is a good thinker. He shares his ideas eagerly and adds interesting insights to discussions. Bryant came up with a new idea for the Choice Time board the other day—Chatting. He describes it this way: "So people can go around and see what other people are doing and chat with them." We're trying it out for a choice—Bryant has signed up for Chatting a few times already!
>
> Though chatting is one of Bryant's favorite things, he is listening better, too. He is becoming more attentive at message time; he regularly

raises his hand to "notice" something on the message. He has been very involved in the *Charlotte's Web* theme. On a few days (maybe tired ones) in the last couple of weeks, his ability to listen has seemed to fall off dramatically, and he has complained of stomachaches.

Bryant seems to enjoy the things that we do during the afternoons when he stays all day. He loves music and art class. He looks happily at books at Quiet Reading Time. He creates "important" stories in his day book, often pictures of a bad guy getting done in. He labels these with assorted letters and reads his story with sound effects included. Jane says that he is interested and involved in the math activities that her group is doing. They have worked on graphing, patterns, free exploration of math manipulatives, and counting.

The stomachaches worry us a bit. Since they are fairly recent, we wonder if they are associated with just too much school. How do you think he is handling the full days?

Our talk that day was inconclusive. Bryant still maintained that school was "pretty good" for him, that he wanted to come to school all day. But all of us were worried about the bellyaches. So far, we had included Thursdays and Fridays as the full days in our week. Soon we would add Wednesdays, the day we had our special phys. ed. class in the afternoon. We wondered if Bryant was hanging on so that he could finally experience gym class! We decided to continue with the all-day schedule for a while longer to see how things developed for Bryant.

In May Bryant began coming to school for a full day on Wednesdays, and indeed, he was thrilled to be going to gym class. His other school-itis symptoms did not disappear, however. He became more antsy at listening times and more lackadaisical about putting pencil to paper. From time to time he still complained of stomachaches. Our Maine weather was finally shaping up into spring, and Bryant was anxious to be outside playing. Bryant's parents eased up on his schedule, and they found opportunities for him to have special days or afternoons off.

More than anything, we all wanted Bryant to be happy in school. We worked at bolstering him up psychologically, finding opportunities for him to move, allowing him plenty of talking and sharing time. Bryant had no specific complaints; he was ready to head out for school in the morning, but he flagged quickly once he got here. It was as if he knew that school was a good place for him in theory, but in practice it just wasn't cutting it. We realized that it was going to be a case of his "hanging in there" until school recessed for the summer, when Bryant could have a couple of months of growing time.

At the end of May, Bryant and I had his first Goal Conference. We decided on one reading goal: "I will work on reading *Mr. Grump*." Bryant enjoyed this book, and he could "read" it from memory almost word-perfectly. I encouraged him to point to the words as he reread it for me, and he found this a chore that was less fun than flipping pages and "reading" fast. The last entry in Bryant's day book for the year showed an airborne figure stuffing a basketball through a hoop. The picture was accompanied by this text: "MCHiEjjWCt" (6/7). Bryant's shared story was in no way connected to his writing!

Though the school year finished up on a rather desultory note in the writing department for Bryant, we were not disheartened. Bryant showed us every day that he was learning in other ways. He was reading a few more words on the message, he was posing questions and solving problems in discussions during math and Investigations, and he was listening to stories with his usual rapt concentration. He went out the classroom door on the last day still loving us and the idea of school. We knew that his family had big travel plans for the summer, and Bryant never looked back. From time to time I kidded Bryant's family, accusing them of providing such a rich family environment for their sons that school couldn't begin to compete! We hoped, though, that a couple of months off for unrestrained fun the way Bryant liked it would bulk him up for the more mundane school stuff in the fall.

However, the early November notes in my day book reveal that Bryant still suffered school doldrums, and that it wasn't smooth sailing for him right away.

Penny's Day Book 11/13

Bryant had a bit of a rough start this year—the days seemed long to him, and he wasn't sure being here all day was the thing. Midway through the first quarter, he complained frequently of stomachaches, of being too sick to listen to message, or to do his writing at Communications Workshop. His complaints lasted about two weeks—he went home on a couple of occasions. His mom was concerned and wondered whether they had made a mistake last year and entered him in school too young. I told her that she had the option of considering him to be a kindergartner again this year, so that he could just come on half days. She was glad to have the option.

Suddenly, though, Bryant's ailments lessened and then stopped. He has been happy during the last few weeks of this first term. He is developing some new friendships. Though he and Ronnie still consider themselves good friends, they do some mean things to each other occasionally. Mostly, it's stuff like "I don't want to play with you today. I'm going to play with so and so." I think Bryant was on the hurting end of this kind of behavior a few times last year, and now he is putting Ronnie through a little hell. Bryant really needed to be by Ronnie's side all the time last year; this year started out the same, but now Bryant is doing more things independently and seeking out other kids to do things with. The relationships among several of the boys in the class are turbulent right now.

I think that Bryant's swing toward happiness here coincided with his gradual realization that he can write. I think this discovery made him realize that his staying all day here was okay!

Bryant's writing breakthrough was gradual. He had started out the year much the way he had ended the previous June. His writing in early September consisted of strings of lowercase and uppercase letters, which did not represent sounds. Sometimes the letters were interspersed with a few known words or names. Soon, though, he seemed to become more aware of what the other children around him were doing at Communications Workshop. He saw them using their dictionaries to find words. He saw them sound-spelling words on their own. He heard them really reading their writing aloud at sharing time. Bryant had many very good stories to tell, and he began to work hard to get them down on paper.

We had realized at the beginning of school that Bryant was becoming more reflective about his learning when we saw the goals for the year that he had discussed and written with his family.

1. Try to spell words myself on homework more often.
2. Read Twig books when I can.
3. Help other kids remember to put the date on their day books.

We were glad that he was thinking about taking the risks and expending the energy to do some of his own spelling. We were pleased that he had selected some appropriate books to practice. And we were gratified to see him taking on a leadership role by planning to help others. Bryant had even signed these goals with his full name, rather than "B.R."!

At first Bryant was not secure enough to attempt sound spelling. He insisted that most words be shown to him or spelled for him in his dictionary. The physical act of writing was arduous for him, and he had many letter reversals. But he left spaces between his words, and he could read his writing: "AFtr we WATCheD th MOVie we will hAVe CAKe it Will Be Goob!" (9/20). Our desire is to create independent writers, so we spell only one word a day for each student. Sensing Bryant's insecurity, we sometimes slipped him an extra word when he came to us with his dictionary in hand, and we worked with him to locate in his dictionary the words he needed. Bryant was thinking about how he could help himself in writing, too. At both of his October Goal Conferences, Bryant specified that his writing goal would be: "I will try to write exciting things."

Bryant worked hard to produce his stories, and he was enthusiastic about sharing them. He always elaborated with extra details when he shared. The listeners often suggested that he write down those details as part of his story, and "putting in lots of details" was one of the characteristics of good writing that the class had identified together during a mini-lesson.

Perhaps Bryant considered these suggestions on a conscious level, or perhaps he was just ready to write. In any case, his stories did begin to get longer. Writing lots of words, many of which could not be found in his dictionary, made sound spelling a necessity. At the beginning of November he adopted these writing goals: "I will try to put lots of details in my story" and "I will work on sound spelling." And through the winter he put these goals into practice. Bryant wrote about topics, both real and imagined, that were close to his heart. "My hAlstsr [hamster] DiD. Curtis YAS [was] Aovr. He ws co [curled] iN A BLL [ball]. I BrEd [buried] hm iN the mDL [middle] AV [of] YM [my] BArD [backyard]. I rmBr [remember] Yr [where] I BeD [buried] hm. I KriD A LAr [long] tAm [time]" (11/14). "Michael JordaN YNt (went) to Bryant Rhodes' is house. TheA [They] PLAD [played] 1 AN 1 [one on one]. It ND [ended] AP [up] tiD [tied]. the AND" (12/22).

We admired the sensitivity of Bryant's writing, and we were glad that he was becoming enthused about his work. He liked to choose writing goals that focused on style: "I will put sound effects in my writing when I need them" and, his favorite, "I will put in exciting things when I need them." We encouraged Bryant to be aware of capitalizing and punctuating appropriately, too. And, now that we had him sound-spelling with abandon, we asked him to check his dictionary for common words from time to time. Bryant was willing to do these tasks to a point; he even set them down as goals. But he was definitely more interested in his message than in mechanics. Checking over his writing to eliminate extraneous uppercase letters was a particularly noxious chore for him.

Though Bryant was writing with more ease, if given a choice he would talk rather than write any day. In December we were finishing up our dinosaur theme, and it was time to decide on research projects. Bryant chose to work alone on a speech about dinosaurs. We supplied him with 3" x 5" cards for note taking, and he closeted himself in the Little Room for several days during Investigations time to work on his speech. He said that he needed to concentrate, and there was too much noise in the classrooms. This was true, since most of the other children were working in groups on projects ranging from plays to dioramas. So Bryant worked happily by himself. The Little Room had been transformed into a dinosaur museum for this theme, and he found it a stimulating nook for speech writing: "I looked around and saw lots of dinosaur things. That helped me think of things to write."

Bryant was poised when he presented his speech to the class. Each of Bryant's four or five notecards contained facts about different dinosaurs. He read from these cards and supplemented the text with facts that he remembered. To end his speech he said: "This is how I think the dinosaurs died. A big comet came down and hit the earth and blacked the sun. All the plants died, so the plant-eaters died. Then the meat-eaters didn't have anything to eat, and they died, too."

When we asked Bryant to evaluate his project, he was self-congratulatory. Some good things about the project were: "I think I did a pretty good job. I thought it was good. Working in the Little Room was good for me." He thought he could have made his project even better by "thinking of more dinosaurs, like the duckbill. It was after a late night, so I couldn't think that straight. I went out to a Pirates game, so I got a splitting headache." Bryant was generally pleased with his efforts; he did what he thought he could manage easily. He wanted to keep it fun.

Bryant was experiencing lots of success in school these days. He was working well in math, making discoveries in our theme work, and writing with enthusiasm. School got even better when he began to read. As is typical of so many children, it happened all of a sudden. I wrote about the event in my day book.

Penny's Day Book—2/20

Bryant has now discovered that he can read. I was beginning to wonder about him. He used to be so interested in books—he'd choose a varied pile and peruse them contentedly last year. This year, however, he has not been so eclectic in his reading—he has been picking out six Twig books each day for the last couple of months. He seems to read these, but he hasn't seemed totally involved or excited at Quiet Reading Time. That has been the case up until a couple of days ago. Now he is hooked on a book: *Pompeii . . . Buried Alive!* He came across it the other day (I don't know how or where), and he was looking at the pictures at Quiet Reading Time. Then he made a discovery—he could read a paragraph on one of the pages! He came over and proudly read the lines to me at Quiet Reading Time. What an event! And this was a long, grown-up kind of book, very different from a Twig book. He finished the period intently perusing this book. The next morning he corralled Justin (one of the older students) before school started and brought out the book. They sat at a table and looked at it together. I had a Goals Conference with Bryant that day, too. Bryant brought the book with him to the conference. He showed me some pictures and talked about it—he also brought a Twig book to read to me. He's been strictly a Twig book guy up until now. I asked him if he'd like to practice *Pompeii . . . Buried Alive!* for a goals book. He seemed a little surprised at the suggestion, but he responded, "Well, sure!" The next day he had the book out again before school—he's plugging away at it with some success. The power of success! Just being able to read those few lines gave him enough confidence to believe that he could read this book. And he can!

Bryant worked on *Pompeii . . . Buried Alive!* for three months. It was the only book he took out for Communications Workshop. He read it through once, and then he read it again and again. Three times he specified *Pompeii . . . Buried Alive!* as the book he would read as his goal book. He read it to friends, made a poster about it, and took it home to read to his family. Bryant was hooked on this book; he "cracked the code" with *Pompeii . . . Buried Alive!* His parents and I talked about the incredible reading phenomenon at our March conference, when I shared these conference notes with them:

Teacher Comments

It's fun to watch when the reading light clicks on, as it has for Bryant recently. Of course, he's had all the background elements poised there for a while, and he *has* been reading. But still, to go from Twig books to *Pompeii . . . Buried Alive!* overnight is pretty dramatic! Bryant is impressed, too! He is also enjoying writing on most days. His vocabulary and sense of story are advanced (we know that from his oral storytelling), and now he is working at getting it all down on paper. It takes a lot of energy! The hard part is thinking a bit about spelling and capital letters and such after creating such a wonderful story. After a bit of discussion each day, Bryant usually agrees to proofread. It's not his favorite thing! He is beginning to spell some common words conventionally.

Bryant is very happy at Choice Time. He usually chooses bricks or blocks or some other hands-on activity, and he values this time for socializing. He has many important comments to add to discussions, and he does participate freely. Recently, we have had to remind Bryant often not to talk when others have the floor. (He told me the other day that he could listen and talk at the same time, which I well believe! The point that we try to impress upon him is that his talking is sometimes distracting others, and that he is not being very considerate of the speaker. He does expect others to listen to him when he is talking! We keep working at it. . . .)

In math Bryant has been working on place value, the concepts of addition and subtraction, and counting and recognizing numbers to 100. He has a good understanding of the concepts. He tends to hurry and to be a little careless on written work. However, he impresses us with his understandings at math workshop. Recently, he worked with a group conducting a class survey of *What is your favorite theme this year?* The children had gathered the data, and they had come together to decide how they would show what they had learned. Bryant right off the bat suggested, "How about if we have a flower and put the theme choices on the petals?" Great idea! He and Shara went off to work on it—the word *Themes* in the middle of six petals, where they recorded their data.

As spring advanced and the year drew to a close, Bryant continued to be responsible for his learning. He seemed to have accepted school as a fact of life. Though maturing wasn't easy for him, he was willing to work at it a bit. On May 9, he wrote in his day book:

> Today is my last day of being 6. Tomorrow I will be 7. Isn't that cool?
> I'm getting tired of being 6.

This entry brought me up short. Bryant did seem older. Suddenly, he saw himself as one of the older kids in the class, someone who could help a first-year student read the choices at sign-up time, someone who could instruct a new student in pumpkin planting techniques, someone who could read and write independently. He was growing up before our eyes, and we had not needed a skills checklist to help us make this discovery.

Looking at the Learners

Another summer passed, and we were back in school again. Rebecca and Bryant were now among our veteran oldest children. We looked forward to our third year with them. Typically, Rebecca bounced back into school on the first day, while Bryant dragged his feet a bit.

School was still a treat for Rebecca. She continued to enthusiastically embrace learning. She was excited to be in my math group, doing "challenging math." She often chose to sign up for Penny's Math at Choice Time, so she could work in her math folder solving problems. Rebecca was dabbling in various genres in her reading, and her writing became more sophisticated. Before Christmas she had published five stories, two of them creatively designed especially for beginning readers. One was a counting book, *The House as Dark as Dark Can Be*. It featured thirteen spooky scenes, beginning with "One little child in the woods" and ending with "13 cupboards . . . And in the cupboards there's 13 ghosts!" (12/4). In another story, *The Black Colt*, Rebecca unleashed the full force of her descriptive powers: "'Naa, naa, naa!' yowled Black Storm, warning the other horses there was a fire in the barn. All the horses were kicking their hooves in fright. Boom, boom it sounded like in the barn. Father woke up and ran outside to see what was all that commotion. Yikes! he yelled. He quickly got all the horses out" (10/30). After Christmas she began to research and write about her Cherokee heritage.

A poem Rebecca wrote early in the fall sums up her excitement about school and her enthusiasm for life in general:

Fall

The leaves turn red.
You rake the leaves.
It starts to get cold.
You jump in the leaves.
You start school.
everyone is happy.
Everyone is joyfull.
When fall comes.

We hope that Rebecca never loses this zeal for learning and life.

School was not such a treat for Bryant, but we saw evidence that he was trying to accept it. During the first few weeks, he complained of stomachaches. "It's not really bad enough that I need to go home, though," he assured us. And Bryant's mother told us that they had discussed the going-back-to-school unease with Bryant. "We acknowledged that he's a boy who might not be perfectly cut out for school, but he thinks he can make it work out pretty well." I confided in Bryant, too, about how hard it was for me to switch gears and get back into the daily school mode each fall.

As the fall weeks went by, Bryant's physical ailments disappeared. Bryant impressed me with his understanding of math concepts and his ability to verbalize his thinking as he, too, joined my math group. He became excited about reading a chapter book about basketball, which he had found on his brother's bookshelf at home. It was truly a big-kid book, and Bryant felt very important reading it. His writing continued to develop stylistically. He spent several weeks writing a story about the adventures of White, the shark, and White's archrival, Long John Silver. He edited and published this story early in December. "There was one man he hated—Long John Silver, who had killed his father. He swore to eat him, tasty or not. The shark was feared by all men." Bryant's absolute favorite part, which he read aloud with gusto, was this section: "White with his teeth and determination and John with his cannons started the mighty battle. White hurled his gigantic body out of the water shouting, 'You weak pathetic blighter!'" Bryant's facility with mechanics, letter formation, and spelling continued to develop slowly, but he proofread less reluctantly. Every week or so we took stock and were surprised to see a gain in one area or another. One day Bryant suddenly had not one backwards *a* in his writing, and one day he spelled *said* and *were* conventionally. Another day we noticed that Bryant's words were well spaced, appearing in straight lines across the page. We saw that he was more prolific in his writing, simply because it had become easier for him physically. Bryant's body was catching up to his mind!

Jane and I wish that we could make school so good that even the Bryants of the world would wholeheartedly embrace it. We can envision that sort of school. Sometimes, in moments of frustration, we tell ourselves that it cannot exist as a public institution, at least not now. Our hands are tied in so many ways, we lament. Our classrooms are too small, our class size is too large, our schedule cannot be flexible enough, our community does not want to spend much money for education, district guidelines are requiring us to waste time on meaningless assessments, and state mandates are often philosophically intrusive. But Bryant and others like him keep us focused on the things we can control. He causes us to continue to question and to refine our practices. He challenges us to keep working to find ways to give everybody "more air" in school.

Shortly after our presentation for the Maine School Management Association, Jane and I presented at another conference for administrators. I was determined to be ready for any sort of attack. Being accosted by that disbelieving veteran kindergarten teacher at the last conference had made a big impression on me. After considerable reflection during the intervening weeks, I now felt prepared to defend our choice-based program to the world. The lesson I did learn, however, was that I would never be prepared for every eventuality. I got another surprise.

At the administrators' conference presentation we were preceded by a university professor who did an overview of the research on multiage education. Perhaps, we thought, the conference organizers believed that their audience needed a greater authority than two classroom teachers to lend credence to the idea of multiage education. The professor summed up his view of the research in four sentences: There isn't any hard data out there that says that multiage education is academically any better for students. There is a slight amount of hard evidence that multiage education promotes better attitudes in students toward school and learning. Most of the research about multiage education should be taken with a grain of salt because it is anecdotal in nature. The research is written by those who are teaching in multiage classrooms and who naturally believe that multiage education is wonderful.

Once again I felt the wind being taken out of my sails. The professor had totally discounted our presentation even before we began! It wasn't fair to be discredited simply because we believed in what we were doing. My anxiety level shot up, and I looked at Jane in panic. Thankfully, she appeared to be as cool as a cucumber. She rolled her eyes and said under her breath, "So, what does this guy know?" And she stood to begin our portion of the workshop.

As she talked, I had time to relax and regroup. I thought about *choice*. These administrators had *chosen* to come here to listen to us speak about our program. I thought about ownership and responsibility. The members of our audience were independent. They could watch and listen to the "anecdotal" evidence we would provide. If they wanted more information, they could refer to the other resources containing both qualitative and quantitative data that we would recommend in our talk. The truly motivated ones would seek out even more material, so they could make informed decisions for themselves. Finally, I thought about trusting the learner to learn. Everyone develops and constructs knowledge at different rates and in different ways. As I got up to speak, I directed a patient smile toward the erudite professor. Who could tell, someday maybe he would be a believer, too.

Bibliography

ACKERMAN, KAREN. [1951] 1988. *Song and Dance Man.* New York: Knopf. Distributed by Random House.

BLAIR, DIANE. 1991. *The Boxcar Children Cookbook.* Morton Grove, IL: A. Whitman and Co.

BRANDT, RON. 1995. "Punished by Rewards? A Conversation with Alfie Kohn." *Educational Leadership* 53 (1): 13–16.

BRAUS, JUDY, ED. 1986. *Nature Scope: Astronomy Adventures.* Washington, DC: National Wildlife Federation.

CHASE, PENELLE, AND JANE DOAN. 1994. *Full Circle: A New Look at Multiage Education.* Portsmouth, NH: Heinemann.

COLE, JOANNA. 1986. *Hungry, Hungry, Sharks.* New York: Random House.

———. 1990. *The Magic School Bus Lost in the Solar System.* New York: Scholastic.

COWLEY, JOY. 1980. *Smarty Pants.* San Diego, CA: The Wright Group.

———. 1986. *Snap!* San Diego, CA: The Wright Group.

———. 1987a. *Mr. Grump.* San Diego, CA: The Wright Group.

———. 1987b. *My Sloppy Tiger.* San Diego, CA: The Wright Group.

CROLL, CAROLYN. 1979. *Too Many Babas.* New York: HarperTrophy.

DECI, EDWARD L., AND CHRISTINE L. CHANDLER. 1986. "The Importance of Motivation for the Future of the LD Field." *Journal of Learning Disabilities* 19 (10): 590.

DECI, E. L., A. J. SCHWARTZ, L. SHEINMAN, AND R. M. RYAN. 1981. "An Instrument to Assess Adult's Orientations Toward Control Versus Autonomy with Children: Reflections on Intrinsic Motivation and Perceived Competence." *Journal of Educational Psychology* 73: 642–50.

DONNELLY, JUDY. 1989. *Moonwalk.* New York: Random House.

DREW, DAVID. 1988a. *Somewhere in the Universe.* Melbourne: Thomas Nelson

Australia. Distributed by Rigby Education, Crystal Lake, IL.

————. 1988b. *Postcards from the Planets*. Melbourne: Thomas Nelson. Distributed by Rigby Education, Crystal Lake, IL.

ELLIOTT, TOMM J. 1993. "Back in the Classroom." *Educational Leadership* 51 (2): 28–30.

GANS, ROMA. 1984. *Rock Collecting*. New York: Harpers.

HASLEY, WILLIAM D., ED. 1977. *School Dictionary*. New York: Macmillan.

HODGES, MARGARET. 1984. *St. George and the Dragon: a Golden Legend*. Boston: Little, Brown.

HOLMES, EMMA E. 1991. "Democracy in Elementary School Classes." *Social Education* 55 (3): 176–77.

KAMII, CONSTANCE. 1982. "Constructivist Education: A Direction for the Twenty-first Century." Paper presented at lecture given in celebration of the 10th Anniversary of Circle Children's Centre, Chicago, IL. 14 January.

————. 1984. "Obedience Is Not Enough." *Young Children*. 39 (4): 11–14.

KASSANS, ZOLA. 1994. "Give Kids Reading Options." *Instructor* 94 (2): 46–48, 51.

KELMAN, ANNA. 1990. "Choices for Children." *Young Children* 45 (3): 42–45.

KOHN, ALFIE. 1993. *Punished by Rewards: The Trouble with Gold Stars, Incentive Plans, A's, Praise, and Other Bribes*. Boston: Houghton Mifflin Company.

KUNHARDT, EDITH. 1987. *Pompeii . . . Buried Alive*. New York: Random House.

LA PLACA, MICHAEL. 1982. *How to Draw Dinosaurs*. NJ: Watermill Press.

LATHAM, ROSS, AND PETER SLOAN. 1986. *Space Shuttle*. Australia: Maurbern Pty Ltd. Distributed by Rigby Education, Crystal Lake, IL.

LOBEL, ARNOLD. 1977. *Mouse Soup*. New York: HarperTrophy.

LONG, KATHLEEN M. 1994. "Wilson Campus School, 1968–77." *Phi Delta Kappan* 546.

MCCLOSKEY, ROBERT. 1948. *Blueberries for Sal*. New York: The Viking Press.

MCGRATH, BARBARA BARBIERI. *M&M's Brand Counting Book*. Watertown, MA: Charlesbridge.

MCMILLAN, BRUCE. 1991. *Play Day: A Book of Terse Verse*. New York: Holiday House.

PERLMUTTER, JANE C., LISA BLOOM, AND LOUISE BURRELL. "Whole Math Through Investigations." 1993. *Childhood Education* (fall): 20–24.

PODENDORF, ILLA. 1981. *Seasons*. Chicago: Children's Press.

PROUDFOOT, MOIRA. 1992. "Teaching Maths Without a Scheme." In *Mathematics with Reason*, edited by Sue Atkinson. Portsmouth, NH: Heinemann, 130–132.

SIMON, SEYMOUR. 1985. *Jupiter*. New York: Morrow.

STANDIFORD, NATALIE. 1989. *The Bravest Dog Ever: The True Story of Balto*. New York: Random House.

STEVENSON, HAROLD W., AND JAMES W. STIGLER. 1992. *The Learning Gap*. New York: Summit Books.

TRESSELT, ALVIN. [1946] 1990. *Rain Drop Splash*. New York: Scholastic.

WARNER, GETRUDE CHANDLER. 1955. *The Boxcar Children*. Chicago: Scott Foresman.

WATTERSON, BILL. 1995. "Calvin and Hobbes." *Boston Sunday Globe*, 16 July.

WHITE, E. B. 1952. *Charlotte's Web*. New York: Harper.

WILDER, LAURA INGALLS. 1953. *Farmer Boy*. New York: Harper.